CROCHET
RAGDOLLS

CROCHET RAGDOLLS

SASCHA BLASE-VAN WAGTENDONK

STACKPOLE BOOKS
Guilford, Connecticut

Published by Stackpole Books
An imprint of The Rowman & Littlefield Publishing Group, Inc.
4501 Forbes Blvd., Ste. 200
Lanham, MD 20706
www.stackpolebooks.com

Distributed by NATIONAL BOOK NETWORK
800-462-6420

First Stackpole edition published in 2020.

Patterns: Sascha Blase-Van Wagtendonk
Graphic design: Femke den Hertog
Photography: Sterstijl, Esther Befort

British Library Cataloguing in Publication Information available

Library of Congress Cataloging-in-Publication Data

Names: Blase-van Wagtendonk, Sascha, author.
Title: Crochet ragdolls / Sascha Blase-Van Wagtendonk.
Other titles: Gehaakte lappenpoppen. English
Description: First edition. | Lanham, MD : Stackpole Books, an imprint of The Rowman & Littlefield Publishing Group, Inc., [2020] | Translation of: Gehaakte lappenpoppen. | Summary: "These crochet ragdolls are specially designed to be huggable lovies for the little ones or loyal playmates for slightly older children. Many of the animals have patterns for both a large 'mom or dad' version and a baby version, including the monkey, frog, cat, bunny, crocodile, dog, hippo, owl, kangaroo, fox, sheep, and penguin. There is even a section on how to make little clothes for them to wear"— Provided by publisher.
Identifiers: LCCN 2019041531 (print) | LCCN 2019041532 (ebook) | ISBN 9780811738835 (hardcover/paperback ; permanent paper) | ISBN 9780811768894 (e-book)
Subjects: LCSH: Crocheting—Patterns. | Rag doll making. | Soft toys.
Classification: LCC TT825 .B5513 2020 (print) | LCC TT825 (ebook) | DDC 746.43/4—dc23
LC record available at https://lccn.loc.gov/2019041531
LC ebook record available at https://lccn.loc.gov/2019041532

∞™ The paper used in this publication meets the minimum requirements of American National Standard for Information Sciences—Permanence of Paper for Printed Library Materials, ANSI/NISO Z39.48-1992.

First Edition

FOREWORD

These ragdolls have been flying off my hook for a while. When I started to crochet these characters, I never expected the family to grow so that they would get their own book!

It is always a pleasure to be able to make a loyal playmate for a special person with some yarn, stuffing, eyes, and a crochet hook!

The dolls have been specially developed to be just as cute and cuddly as a cuddle cloth, but the unique shape also allows older children to play with these toys and put their imagination into them.

There is so much variety in the characters—something for everyone. The animals are suitable for boys and girls and are easy to personalize with color selection. You'll find an awesome robot as a super cool counterpart to the super cute little princess!

Most of the dolls are pretty easy to crochet. A few of the figures are slightly more difficult due to the color changes, but changing colors is explained in the "Tips & Tricks" chapter (page xvi), and once you do it a few times, it is no trouble at all.

Have fun crocheting these adorable ragdolls!

Love, Sascha

www.alasascha.com | Facebook: AlaSascha

CONTENTS

CROCHET STITCHES

Chain	ch
Slip stitch	sl st
Single crochet	sc
Half double crochet	hdc
Double crochet	dc
Triple crochet	tr
Single crochet 2 together	sc2tog
Double crochet 2 together	dc2tog
Front post double crochet	fpdc
Back post double crochet	bpdc

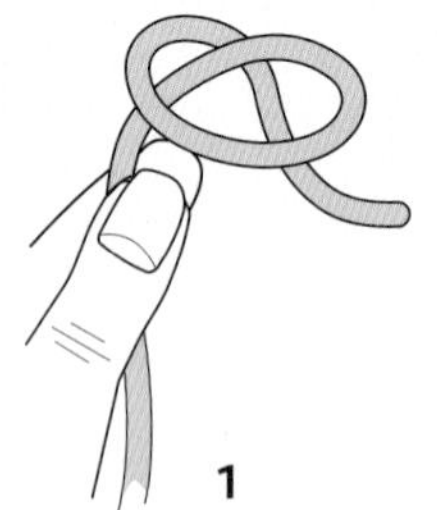
1

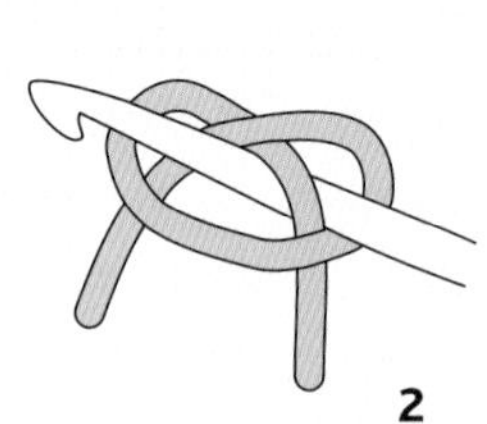
2

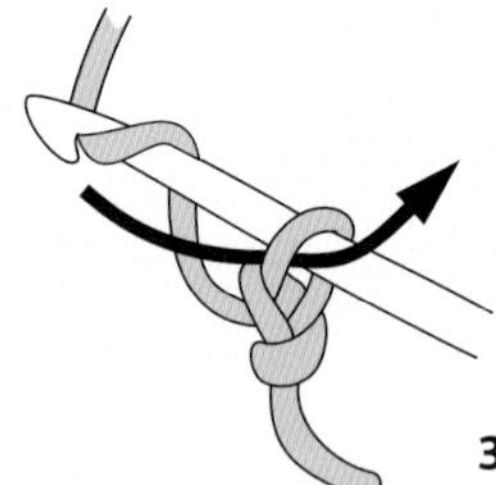
3

SLIPKNOT

Your crochet (usually) starts with a slipknot and chain stitches. Lay the loose end of your thread over the thread that is attached to the ball of yarn, and then fold it down behind the loop (1). Now insert your crochet hook into the ring and behind the end, then forward again (2). Tighten the thread, and you have made a slipknot. You can now work the setup chain by hooking through the loop on your hook (3).

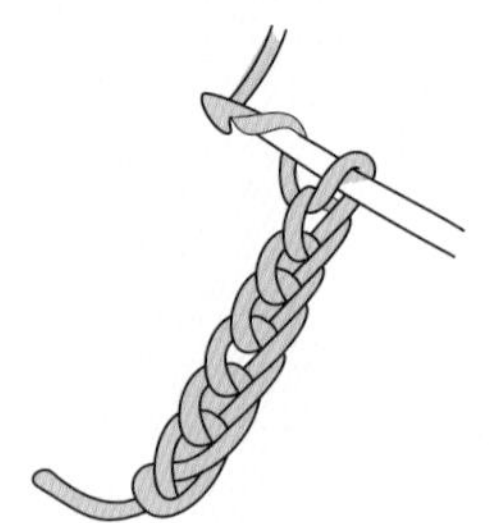

CHAIN (ch)

Wrap the working yarn from back to front over the crochet hook. Now pull the yarn through the loop on your hook, and you have made a chain stitch. Repeat for the desired number of chains.

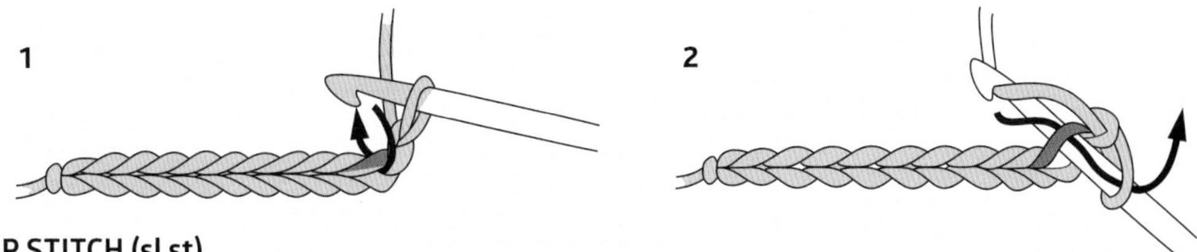

SLIP STITCH (sl st)
Insert the crochet hook from the front to the back (1) and then under the thread so that the working yarn is over your crochet hook (2). Now pull the yarn through the 2 loops on your hook, and you have made a slip stitch.

SINGLE CROCHET (sc)
Insert the crochet hook from the front to the back (1) and wrap the working yarn over the hook from back to front. Now pull the yarn through the stitch. Wrap the yarn over the hook from back to front again and pull this through the 2 loops on your hook (2), and you have made a single crochet.

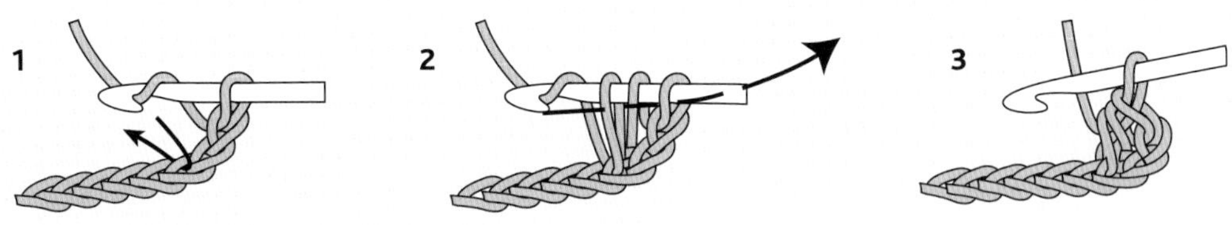

HALF DOUBLE CROCHET (hdc)
Wrap the working yarn from back to front over the crochet hook (1). Insert the crochet hook from the front to the back, wrap the working yarn over the hook from back to front, and then pull the yarn through the stitch. Make another wrap and pass it through the 3 loops on your hook (2), and you have made a half double crochet (3).

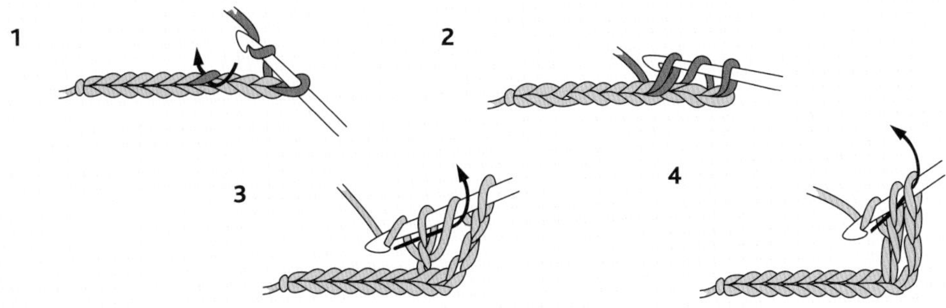

DOUBLE CROCHET (dc)
Wrap the working yarn from back to front over the crochet hook (1). Insert the crochet hook from the front to the back, wrap the yarn over the hook, and then pull the yarn through the stitch (2). Make another wrap and pass it through 2 of the loops on your hook (3). Then make another wrap and pull it through the last 2 loops on your hook (4), and you have made a double crochet.

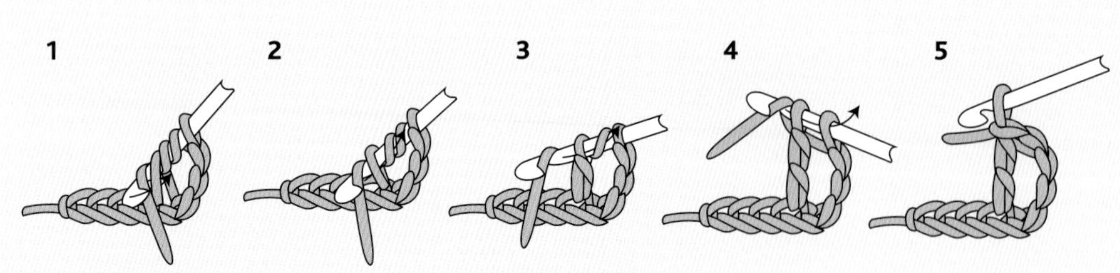

TRIPLE CROCHET (tr)

Wrap the yarn around the crochet hook 2 times from back to front. Insert the crochet hook from the front to the back, make a wrap and pull the yarn through the stitch (1), *make another wrap and pull it through 2 of the loops on your hook* (2), repeat from * to * 2 more times (3 and 4), and you have made a triple crochet (5).

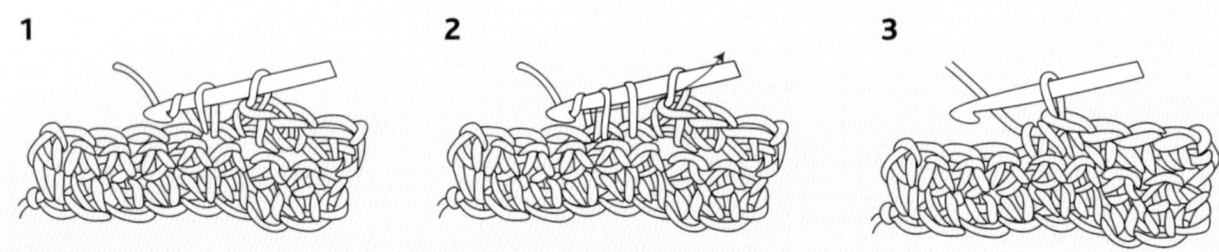

SINGLE CROCHET TOGETHER (sctog)

Insert the crochet hook from front to back in the next stitch. Wrap the working yarn from back to front over the crochet hook and pull the yarn through the stitch (1). Repeat these steps for the next stitch (or multiple stitches that you want to join). Finally, make a wrap and pull it through all the loops on your hook (2). You now have crocheted several stitches together, decreasing the total stitch count (3).

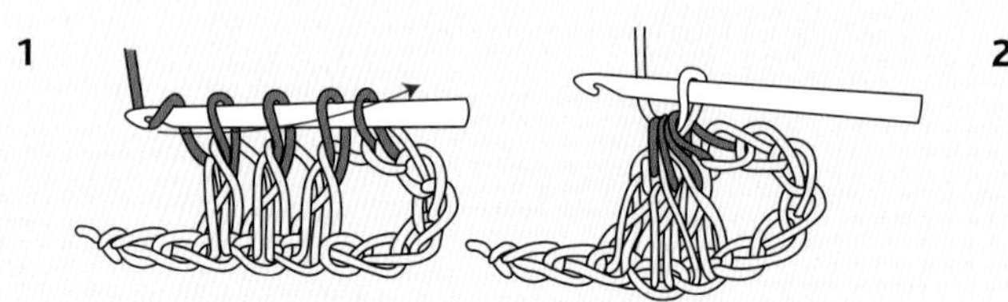

DOUBLE CROCHET TOGETHER (dctog)

Wrap the working yarn from back to front over the crochet hook. Insert the crochet hook from the front to the back in the next stitch. Make a wrap and pull it through the stitch, and then make another wrap and pull it through 2 of the loops on your hook. Repeat these steps for the next or possibly several stitches that you want to join. Finally, make a wrap and pull it through all the loops on your hook (1). You have now double crocheted several stitches together to make 1 stitch (2).

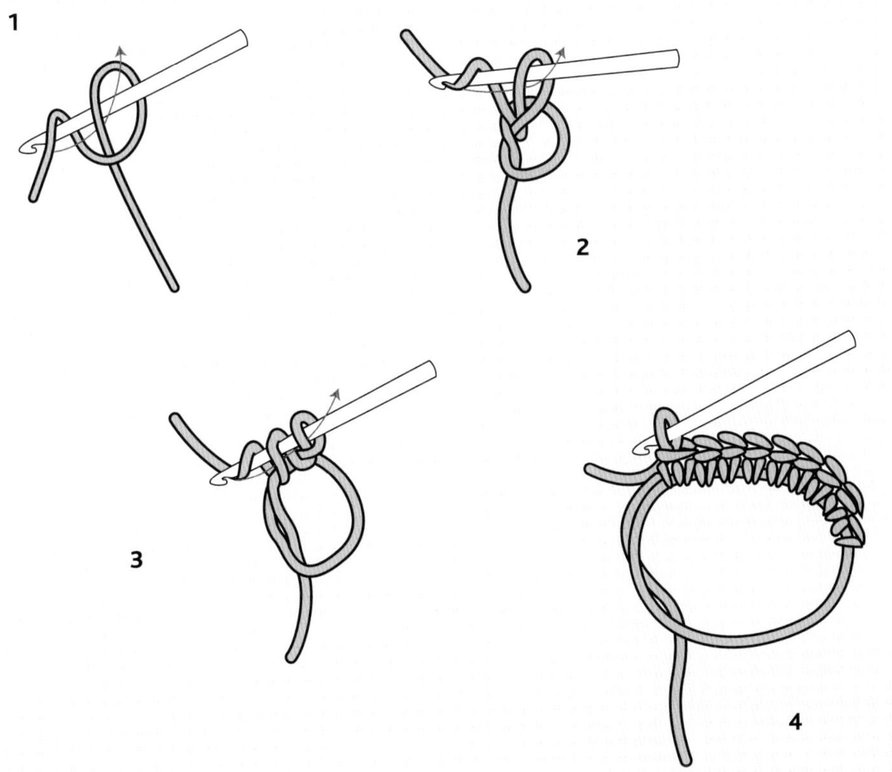

MAGIC RING

Make a circle of the yarn by folding the loose end of the yarn behind the yarn attached to the skein. Now insert your crochet hook into the ring. Wrap the working yarn over your hook and pull the yarn through the ring (1). Hook 1 chain to secure the ring (2).

Then hook the number of stitches in the ring as indicated in the pattern. Make sure that you hook around the strands of both the ring and the loose end of the yarn (3 and 4). When you have the desired number of stitches, pull the loose end tightly to close the ring. Then continue in pattern.

YARN CHOICES

All the sample animals are crocheted with Scheepjes Stone Washed. This is a yarn with a special soft, tonal appearance with few equivalents. However, you can use other yarns and brands to crochet the dolls. On this page and the following, you'll see examples of the same pattern crocheted in different yarns. Try any of these yarns, or make your own choices from your stash or local craft store.

All these ragdolls are crocheted with a US size D-3 (3 mm) crochet hook, but, as you can see, each yarn has its own effect and the finished ragdolls also vary in size!

1 Scheepjes Stone Washed: recommended hook size US D-3–F-5 (3–4 mm); 78% cotton, 22% acrylic; 1.75 oz. (50 g); 142 yd. (130 m) per ball. This yarn makes the ragdoll 14.2 in. (36 cm) high and the body 5.9 in. (15 cm) wide.

2 Annell Miami or Scheepjes Soft Fun: recommended hook size US D-3–E-4 (3–3.5 mm); 60% cotton, 40% acrylic; 1.75 oz. (50 g); 153 yd. (140 m) per ball. This yarn makes the ragdoll 15 in. (38 cm) high and the body 6.3 in. (16 cm) wide.

3 SMC Merino Extrafine 120: recommended hook size US D-3–F-5 (3–4 mm); 100% new milled wool; 1.75 oz. (50 g); 131.2 yd. (120 m) per ball. This yarn makes the ragdoll 13.4 in. (34 cm) high and the body 5.1 in. (13 cm) wide.

4 Lammy Jeans: recommended hook size US E-4–G-6 (3.5–4 mm); 100% cotton; 1.75 oz. (50 g); 153 yd. (140 m) per ball. This yarn makes the ragdoll 14.2 in. (36 cm) high and the body 5.5 in. (14 cm) wide.

5 SMC Catania Grande: recommended hook size US G-6–H-8 (4–5 mm); 100% cotton; 1.75 oz. (50 g); 68.9 yd. (63 m) per ball. This yarn makes the ragdoll 16.9 in. (43 cm) high and the body 6.3 in. (16 cm) wide. This yarn is thicker than the other yarns, so you can also use a slightly thicker crochet hook US size E-4/F-5/G-6 (3.5–5 mm), and your ragdoll will become a little larger.

1. You crochet a lot of parts in continuous rounds; it is therefore useful to use a stitch marker.

2. To change colors, work the last step of the stitch before the color change. For example, if the last stitch in the old color is a single crochet, work the last wrap over the hook that you then pull through 2 loops.

3. With a number of the patterns, you change colors regularly. Instead of fastening off every time, carry the unused color along. You do this by holding the color that you are not using along the top of the stitches to be crocheted and hooking around it so that it is encased by the working color and hidden on the back of the work.

4. You can add sounds to the ragdolls to give them an extra play element. For example, put a squeaker in the head of the mouse, a bell in the head of the cat, a rattle bead in a hand, or a sheet of crisp plastic in the body.

5. Safety eyes should only be used on ragdolls meant for children over the age of three. When making a ragdoll for a younger child, please replace with crocheted or embroidered eyes for optimal safety.

6. Here are some tips for making the body:
   - The body is worked in the round. You'll start with a chain on which you'll crochet along both sides to begin the top of the body.
   - You'll always start with a ch2, which doesn't count as the first dc, so the actual first dc will be made in the same stitch as the ch2.
   - Your increases should stack on top of each other.
   - Depending on how tight you crochet, the body may twist a little. But in the end, you can fold it flat in line with the increases and sew in place.
   - When working a two-color body, you'll notice that the increases of the second color will be made only on one side. This is because when you crochet in the round, your stitches automatically turn to the right, so this will make the belly look even.

SKILL LEVELS

● Beginner
●● Advanced beginner
●●● Intermediate
●●●● Advanced intermediate
●●●●● Advanced

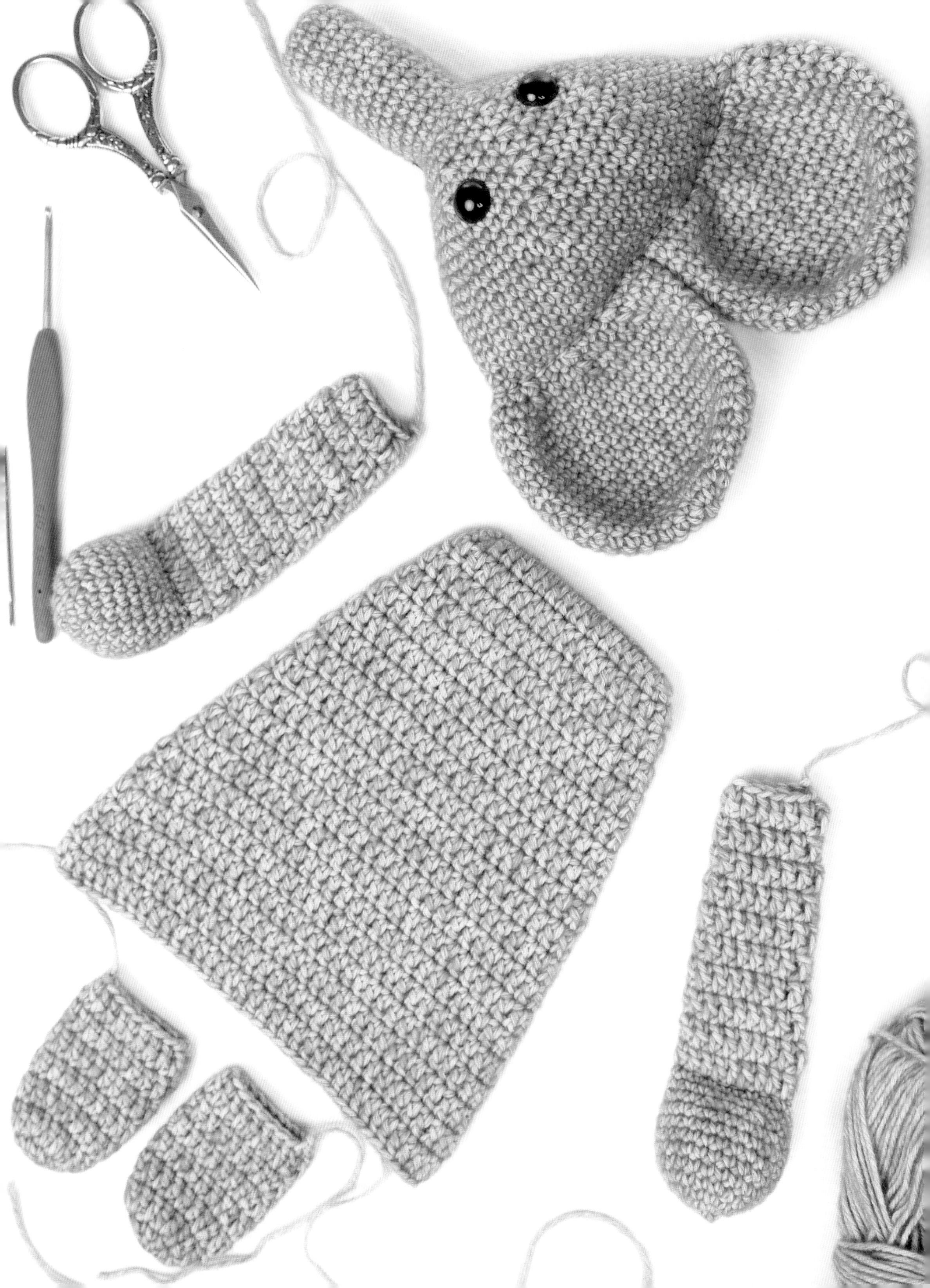

ASSEMBLY

The dolls all have the same basic construction. The patterns themselves describe in detail how to assemble each specific one, but here are some general instructions including photos.

CROCHETING THE HEAD

All the heads are crocheted in the round, but in a number of different ways. The simplest patterns start with a magic ring or a chain around which you then continue to crochet in the round. Another way is to start crocheting two eyes or two ears that you then hook together in one row to form the top of the head. Or you can start with the top component, such as the eyes or a bun, and then make a chain between or beside it; then you continue to crochet around all stitches.

PLACING THE LEGS AND TAIL (IF ONE)

It is very important that you fold the body so that the belly is in the middle. This is especially important with the dolls that have a white belly. Take the body and place both legs (and possibly the tail) between the two layers at the bottom; then sew the bottom of the body with the remaining yarn and at the same time attach the parts.

1

2

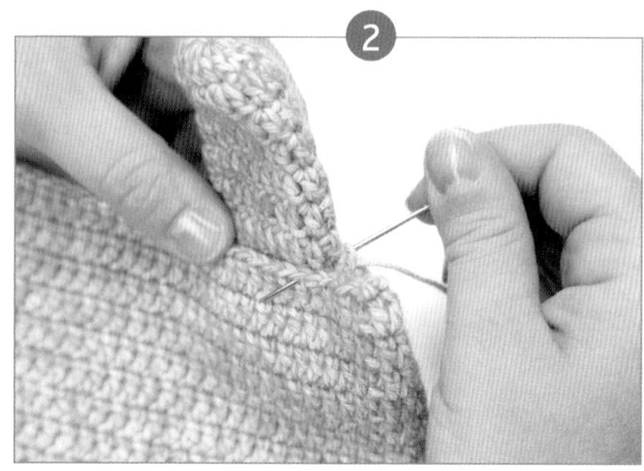

3

ATTACHING THE ARMS

Sew an arm on either side of the upper rounds of the body. The precise rounds will be indicated in the pattern.

1

2

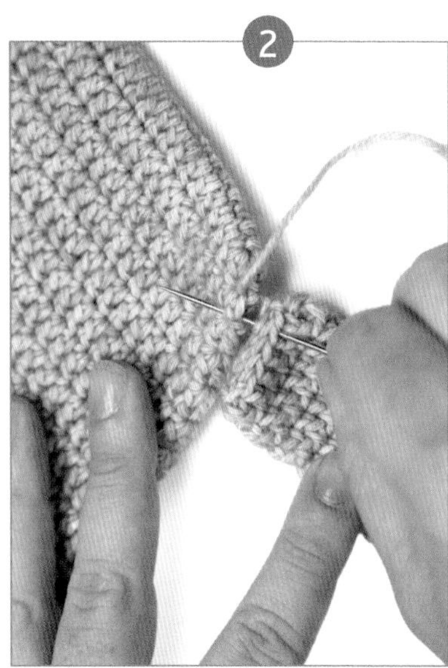

3

ATTACHING THE HEAD

Finally, sew the back of the head to the body through both layers. The precise rounds will be indicated in the pattern.

1

2

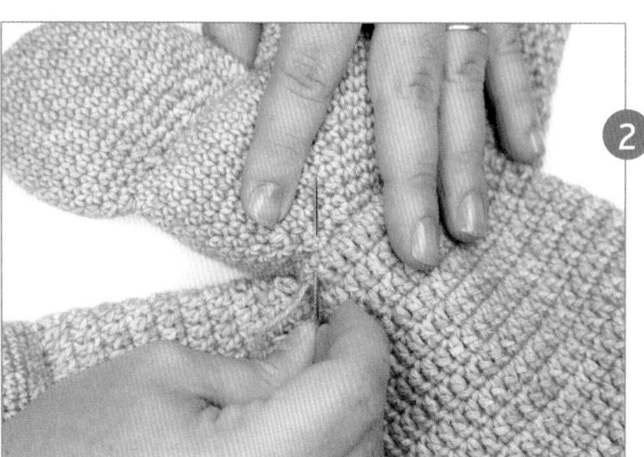

3

ANIMAL FAMILIES

BUNNY

This bunny loves to sniff and cuddle.

DIMENSIONS

18.1 in. (46 cm) high (with ears) and 6.7 in. (17 cm) wide

MATERIALS

DK #3 lightweight yarn (sample shown in Scheepjes Stone Washed):

- gray (Smokey Quartz): 251.5 yd. (230 m)
- white (Moon Stone): 142.2 yd. (130 m)

Crochet hook: US size D-3 (3 mm)

Black and brown safety eyes, 15 mm

Safety nose, 15 mm wide

Fiberfill stuffing

Yarn needle and scissors

DIFFICULTY LEVEL

EARS (MAKE 2)

Rnd 1: With gray, start with a magic ring, ch2, 6dc in the ring, sl st in first dc. (6)
Rnd 2: Ch2 (doesn't count as first stitch now and throughout), 2dc in each stitch around, sl st in first dc. (12)
Rnd 3: Ch2, *dc1, 2dc in next*, repeat from * to * around, sl st in first dc. (18)
Rnd 4: Ch2, *dc2, 2dc in next*, repeat from * to * around, sl st in first dc. (24)
Rnd 5–Rnd 7: Ch2, dc1 in each stitch around, sl st in first dc. (24)
Rnd 8: Ch2, *dc2, dc2tog*, repeat from * to * around, sl st in first dc. (18)
Rnd 9–Rnd 16: Ch2, dc1 in each stitch around, sl st in first dc. (18)
Cut yarn of first ear, but don't cut yarn of second ear because you'll continue working with it to form the top of the head.

HEAD

Rnd 1: While holding the second ear, take the first ear and continue single crocheting in each stitch around (18 sc); continue single crocheting in each stitch around of second ear (18 sc), making a total of 36 sc.
Rnd 2: *Sc5, 2sc in next*, repeat from * to * around. (42)
Rnd 3: *Sc6, 2sc in next*, repeat from * to * around. (48)
Rnd 4: *Sc7, 2sc in next*, repeat from * to * around. (54)
Rnd 5–Rnd 11: Sc1 in each stitch around. (54) You can cut the gray yarn.
Rnd 12–Rnd 14: With white sc1 in each stitch around. (54)
Rnd 15: *Sc7, sc2tog*, repeat from * to * around. (48)
Rnd 16: *Sc6, sc2tog*, repeat from * to * around. (42)
Rnd 17: *Sc5, sc2tog*, repeat from * to * around. (36)
Rnd 18: *Sc4, sc2tog*, repeat from * to * around. (30)
Rnd 19: *Sc3, sc2tog*, repeat from * to * around. (24)
Rnd 20: *Sc2, sc2tog*, repeat from * to * around. (18)
Take the safety eyes and attach them to the head between Rnd 9 and Rnd 10, and attach the safety nose between the eyes between Rnd 13 and Rnd 14. Now take a piece of gray yarn and sew across the top of the head to close off the ears so they won't be stuffed. Stuff the head. Cut the white yarn.
Rnd 21: *Sc1, sc2tog* repeat from * to * around. (12)
Cut a long tail and sew the seam closed.
Lastly, embroider three whiskers on each side of the nose, as shown in the picture.

BODY

Rnd 1: With gray ch18, 1dc in third ch from hook, dc14, 3dc in last, continue along other side of chains, dc15, 3dc in last, sl st in first dc. (36)
Rnd 2: Ch2 (doesn't count as first stitch now and throughout), dc3, **with white** dc11, **with gray** dc3, 2dc in next, dc17, 2dc in next, sl st in first dc. (38)
Rnd 3: With gray ch2, dc3, **with white** dc12, **with gray** dc3, 2dc in next, dc18, 2dc in next, sl st in first dc. (40)
Rnd 4: With gray ch2, dc3, **with white** dc13, **with gray** dc3, 2dc in next, dc19, 2dc in next, sl st in first dc. (42)
Rnd 5: With gray ch2, dc3, **with white** dc14, **with gray** dc3, 2dc in next, dc20, 2dc in next, sl st in first dc. (44)
Rnd 6: With gray ch2, dc3, **with white** dc15, **with gray** dc3, 2dc in next, dc21, 2dc in next, sl st in first dc. (46)
Rnd 7: With gray ch2, dc3, **with white** dc16, **with gray** dc3, 2dc in next, dc22, 2dc in next, sl st in first dc. (48)
Rnd 8: With gray ch2, dc3, **with white** dc17, **with gray** dc3, 2dc in next, dc23, 2dc in next, sl st in first dc. (50)
Rnd 9: With gray ch2, dc3, **with white** dc18, **with gray** dc3, 2dc in next, dc24, 2dc in next, sl st in first dc. (52)
Rnd 10: With gray ch2, dc3, **with white** dc19, **with gray** dc3, 2dc in next, dc25, 2dc in next, sl st in first dc. (54)
Rnd 11: With gray ch2, dc3, **with white** dc20, **with gray** dc3, 2dc in next, dc26, 2dc in next, sl st in first dc. (56)
Rnd 12: With gray ch2, dc3, **with white** dc21, with gray dc3, 2dc in next, dc27, 2dc in next, sl st in first dc. (58)
Rnd 13: With gray ch2, dc3, **with white** dc22, **with gray** dc3, 2dc in next, dc28, 2dc in next, sl st in first dc. (60)
Rnd 14: With gray ch2, dc3, **with white** dc23, **with gray** dc3, 2dc in next, dc29, 2dc in next, sl st in first dc. (62)
Rnd 15: With gray ch2, dc3, **with white** dc24, **with gray** dc3, 2dc in next, dc30, 2dc in next, sl st in first dc. (64)
Rnd 16: With gray ch2, dc3, **with white** dc25, **with gray** dc3, 2dc in next, dc31, 2dc in next, sl st in first dc. (66)
Rnd 17: With gray ch2, dc3, **with white** dc26, **with gray** dc3, 2dc in next, dc32, 2dc in next, sl st in first dc. (68)
Rnd 18: With gray ch2, dc3, **with white** dc27, **with gray** dc3, 2dc in next, dc33, 2dc in next, sl st in first dc. (70)
Rnd 19: With gray ch2, dc3, **with white** dc28, **with gray** dc3, 2dc in next, dc34, 2dc in next, sl st in first dc. (72)
Rnd 20: With gray ch2, dc3, **with white** dc29, **with gray** dc3, 2dc in next, dc35, 2dc in next, sl st in first dc. (74)
Cut a long tail to close the body in the end.

ARMS (MAKE 2)

Rnd 1: With white, start with a magic ring, 6sc in the loop. (6)
Rnd 2: 2sc in each stitch around. (12)
Rnd 3: *Sc1, 2sc in next*, repeat from * to * around. (18)
Rnd 4: *Sc2, 2sc in next*, repeat from * to * around. (24)
Rnd 5–Rnd 9: Sc in each stitch around. (24)
Rnd 10: *Sc2, sc2tog*, repeat from * to * around. (18)
Rnd 11–Rnd 12: Sc in each stitch around. (18)
Cut a long tail of the white yarn; you'll need it after Rnd 14.
Rnd 13: With gray sl st 1, ch2 (doesn't count as first stitch now and throughout), dc in each stitch around, sl st in first dc. (18)
Rnd 14: Ch2, dc2tog, dc in each stitch around, sl st in first dc. (17)
At this point, stuff the hand, take the yarn from Rnd 12, and sew across arm between Rnd 12 and Rnd 13.
Rnd 15: Ch2, dc in each stitch around, sl st in first dc. (17)
Rnd 16: Ch2, dc2tog, dc in each stitch around, sl st in first dc. (16)
Rnd 17: Ch2, dc in each stitch around, sl st in first dc. (16)
Rnd 18: Ch2, dc2tog, dc in each stitch around, sl st in first dc. (15)
Rnd 19: Ch2, dc in each stitch around, sl st in first dc. (15)
Rnd 20: Ch2, dc2tog, dc in each stitch around, sl st in first dc. (14)
Rnd 21: Ch2, dc in each stitch around, sl st in first dc. (14)
Rnd 22: Ch2, dc2tog, dc in each stitch around, sl st in first dc. (13)
Cut a long tail to attach arms to body later.

LEGS (MAKE 2)

Rnd 1: With white, start with a magic ring, ch2, 12dc in the loop, sl st in first dc. (12)
Rnd 2: Ch2, *dc1, 2dc in next*, repeat from * to * around, sl st in first dc. (18)
Rnd 3: Ch2, dc in each stitch around, sl st in first dc. (18)
Rnd 4–Rnd 7: With gray ch2, dc in each stitch around, sl st in first dc. (18)
Cut yarn and weave in ends.

PUTTING IT ALL TOGETHER

- Take the body and place both legs between the bottom two layers. Take the remaining yarn from the body and sew across the seam, with legs in between, to close and at the same time attach legs.
- Sew both arms to each side of the body between Rnd 2 and Rnd 4.
- Take the head and sew Rnd 15 of the head to Rnd 1 of the body.

BABY BUNNY

Kids love these little bunnies.

DIMENSIONS

5.5 in. (14 cm) long (not including ears) and 3.9 in. (10 cm) wide

MATERIALS

DK #3 lightweight yarn (sample shown in Scheepjes Stone Washed):
- pink (Red Jasper): 109.4 yd. (100 m)
- light pink (Rose Quartz): 65.6 yd. (60 m)

Crochet hook: US D-3 (3 mm)
Black safety eyes, 12 mm
Pink safety nose, 8 mm
Fiberfill stuffing
Yarn needle and scissors

DIFFICULTY LEVEL

EARS (MAKE 2)

Rnd 1: With pink, start with a magic ring, ch2, 6dc in the loop, sl st in first dc. (6)
Rnd 2: Ch2 (doesn't count as first dc), 2dc in each stitch around, sl st in first dc. (12)
Rnd 3: Ch2, *dc1, 2dc in next*, repeat from * to * around, sl st in first dc. (18)
Rnd 4–Rnd 5: Ch2, dc in each stitch around, sl st in first dc. (18)
Rnd 6: Ch2, *dc1, dc2tog*, repeat from * to * around, sl st in first dc. (12)
Rnd 7–Rnd 11: Ch2, dc1 in each stitch around, sl st in first dc. (12) Cut the yarn of the first ear, but don't cut the yarn of the second ear. You'll continue to work with it to make the top of the head.

HEAD

Rnd 1: With pink, while holding the second ear, take the first ear and single crochet in each stitch around (12), continue working sc1 in each stitch around of second ear (12), making a total of 24.
Rnd 2: *Sc3, 2sc in next*, repeat from * to * around. (30)
Rnd 3: *Sc4, 2sc in next*, repeat from * to * around. (36)
Rnd 4–Rnd 7: Sc1 in each stitch around. (36) You can cut the pink yarn.
Rnd 8–Rnd 9: With light pink sc1 in each stitch around. (36)
Rnd 10: *Sc4, sc2tog*, repeat from * to * around. (30)
Rnd 11: *Sc3, sc2tog*, repeat from * to * around. (24)
Rnd 12: *Sc2, sc2tog*, repeat from * to * around. (18)
Take the safety eyes and attach them to the head between Rnd 5 and Rnd 6 (ear not included) with 7 stitches in between, but make sure that the first stitches (where you see the color change) are on the back. Attach the safety nose between Rnd 8 and Rnd 9 and between the eyes. Now take a piece of pink yarn and sew across the top of the head to close off the ears so they won't be stuffed. Stuff the head.
Rnd 13: *Sc1, sc2tog*, repeat from * to * around. (12)
Cut a long tail and sew the seam closed.

BODY

Rnd 1: With pink ch13, dc1 in 3rd ch from hook, dc9, 3dc in last, continue along other side of chains, dc10, 3dc in last, sl st in first dc. (26)
Rnd 2: Ch2 (doesn't count as first stitch now and throughout), *dc12, 2dc in next* repeat from * to * one more time, sl st in first dc. (28)
Rnd 3: Ch2, dc3, **with light pink** dc7, **with pink** dc3, 2dc in next, dc13, 2dc in next, sl st in first dc. (30)
Rnd 4: Ch2, dc3, **with light pink** dc8, **with pink** dc3, 2dc in next, dc14, 2dc in next, sl st in first dc. (32)
Rnd 5: Ch2, dc3, **with light pink** dc9, **with pink** dc3, 2dc in next, dc15, 2dc in next, sl st in first dc. (34)
Rnd 6: Ch2, dc3, **with light pink** dc10, **with pink** dc3, 2dc in next, dc16, 2dc in next, sl st in first dc. (36)
Rnd 7: Ch2, dc3, **with light pink** dc11, **with pink** dc3, 2dc in next, dc17, 2dc in next, sl st in first dc. (38)
Rnd 8: Ch2, dc3, **with light pink** dc12, **with pink** dc3, 2dc in next, dc18, 2dc in next, sl st in first dc. (40)
Rnd 9: Ch2, dc3, **with light pink** dc13, **with pink** dc3, 2dc in next, dc19, 2dc in next, sl st in first dc. (42)
Rnd 10: Ch2, dc3, **with light pink** dc14, **with pink** dc3, 2dc in next, dc20, 2dc in next, sl st in first dc. (44)
Rnd 11: Ch2, dc3, **with light pink** dc15, **with pink** dc3, 2dc in next, dc21, 2dc in next, sl st in first dc. (46) Cut the light pink yarn and weave in the end.
Rnd 12: Ch2, *dc22, ch14, dc1 in 3rd ch from hook, dc1 in each of the remaining 11 chains, 2dc in next stitch of Rnd 11*, repeat from * to * one more time, sl st in first dc.
Cut a long tail to close the body later.

ARMS (MAKE 2)

Rnd 1: With pink, start with a magic ring, sc6 in the loop. (6)
Rnd 2: 2sc in each stitch around. (12)
Rnd 3: *Sc1, 2sc in next*, repeat from to * around. (18)
Rnd 4–Rnd 5: Sc1 in each stitch around. (18)
Rnd 6: *Sc1, sc2tog*, repeat from * to * around. (12)
Rnd 7: Sc1 in each stitch around. (12)
Rnd 8: Sl st 1, ch2 (doesn't count as first stitch now and throughout), dc1 in each stitch around, sl st in first dc. (12)
Rnd 9: Ch2, dc2tog, dc1 in each stitch around, sl st in first dc. (11)
At this point, stuff the hand and sew across arm between Rnd 7 and Rnd 8.
Rnd 10: Ch2, dc1 in each stitch around, sl st in first dc. (11)
Rnd 11: Ch2, dc2tog, dc1 in each stitch around, sl st in first dc. (10)
Rnd 12: Ch2, dc1 in each stitch around, sl st in first dc. (10)
Rnd 13: Ch2, dc2tog, dc1 in each stitch around, sl st in first dc. (9)
Cut a long tail to attach arms to body later.

PUTTING IT ALL TOGETHER

- Fold the body in line with the increases to make the belly straight and sew closed with the remaining yarn. Tie a knot in the corners to form the feet.
- Sew an arm to each side of the body in Rnd 1 and Rnd 2.
- Finally, take the head and sew Rnd 10 (ears not included) to Rnd 1 of the body.

CROCODILE

DIMENSIONS

11 in. (28 cm) high and 6.7 in. (17 cm) wide

MATERIALS

DK #3 lightweight yarn (sample shown in Scheepjes Stone Washed):
- green (Canada Jade): 284.3 yd. (260 m)

Crochet hook: US size D-3 (3 mm)
Brown and black safety eyes, 15 mm
Small amount of fiberfill stuffing
Yarn needle and scissors

DIFFICULTY LEVEL

EYES (MAKE 2)

Rnd 1: Start with a magic ring, 6sc in the loop. (6)
Rnd 2: 2sc in each stitch around. (12)
Rnd 3: *Sc1, 2sc in next*, repeat from * to * around. (18)
Rnd 4: *Sc2, 2sc in next*, repeat from * to * around. (24)
Rnd 5–Rnd 8: Sc1 in each stitch around. (24)
For the first eye, cut the yarn and secure the end. For the second eye, don't cut the yarn and continue with head instructions.

HEAD

The eyes will be connected to start the top of the head.
Rnd 1: Take both eyes, continue with second eye, sc11, take first eye and sc next stitch of second eye and first stitch of first eye together, sc22, sc next stitch of first eye and next stitch of second eye together, sc11. (46)
Rnd 2: Sc1 in each stitch around. (46)
Rnd 3: 2sc in first stitch, sc23, 2sc in next stitch, sc21. (48)
Rnd 4: 2sc in each of first 2 stitches, sc23, 2sc in each of next 2 stitches, sc21. (52)
Rnd 5: 2sc in each of first 4 stitches, sc23, 2sc in each of next 4 stitches, sc21. (60)
Rnd 6–Rnd 7: Sc1 in each stitch around. (60)
Rnd 8: Sc4, sc2tog, sc28, sc2tog, sc24. (58)
Rnd 9: Sc4, sc2tog, sc27, sc2tog, sc23. (56)
Rnd 10: Sc4, sc2tog, sc26, sc2tog, sc22. (54)
Rnd 11: Sc4, sc2tog, sc25, sc2tog, sc21. (52)
Rnd 12: Sc4, sc2tog, sc24, sc2tog, sc20. (50)
Rnd 13: Sc4, sc2tog, sc23, sc2tog, sc19. (48)
Rnd 14: Sc4, sc2tog, sc22, sc2tog, sc18. (46)
Rnd 15: Sc4, sc2tog, sc21, sc2tog, sc17. (44)
Rnd 16: Sc4, sc2tog, sc20, sc2tog, sc16. (42)
Rnd 17: Sc4, sc2tog, sc19, sc2tog, sc15. (40)
Rnd 18: Sc4, sc2tog, sc18, sc2tog, sc14. (38)
Rnd 19: Sc4, sc2tog, sc17, sc2tog, sc13. (36)
Rnd 20: Sc4, sc2tog, sc16, sc2tog, sc12. (34)
Rnd 21: Sc4, sc2tog, sc15, sc2tog, sc11. (32)
Rnd 22: Sc4, sc2tog, sc14, sc2tog, sc10. (30)
Rnd 23: Sc1 in each stitch around. (30)
Rnd 24: Sc3, sc2tog, sc13, sc2tog, sc10. (28)
Rnd 25: Sc1 in each stitch around. (28)

Rnd 26: Sc4, hdc1, dc3, hdc1, sc1, sl st1, sc1, hdc1, dc3, hdc1, sc1, hdc1, dc3, hdc1, sc1, sl st1, sc1, hdc1, dc1. (28)
Rnd 27: Dc2, hdc1, sc1, hdc1, dc3, hdc1, sc1, sl st1, sc1, hdc1, dc3, hdc1, sc1, hdc1, dc3, hdc1, sc1, sl st1, sc1, hdc1, dc1. (28)
Rnd 28: Dc2, hdc1, sc1, sl st 1. This is where this rnd ends. Cut a long tail. Now attach a safety eye to each side between Rnd 8 of the eyes and Rnd 1 of the head; stuff the head and sew the seam for the mouth closed.

BODY

Rnd 1: Ch20, dc in third ch from hook, dc16, 3dc in last, continue along other side of chains, dc17, 3dc in last, sl st in first dc. (40)
Rnd 2: Ch2 (doesn't count as first stitch now and throughout), *dc19, 2dc in next*, repeat from * to * one more time, sl st in first dc. (42)
Rnd 3: Ch2, *dc20, 2dc in next*, repeat from * to * one more time, sl st in first dc. (44)
Rnd 4: Ch2, *dc21, 2dc in next*, repeat from * to * one more time, sl st in first dc. (46)
Rnd 5: Ch2, *dc22, 2dc in next*, repeat from * to * one more time, sl st in first dc. (48)
Rnd 6: Ch2, *dc23, 2dc in next*, repeat from * to * one more time, sl st in first dc. (50)
Rnd 7: Ch2, *dc24, 2dc in next*, repeat from * to * one more time, sl st in first dc. (52)
Rnd 8: Ch2, *dc25, 2dc in next*, repeat from * to * one more time, sl st in first dc. (54)
Rnd 9: Ch2, *dc26, 2dc in next*, repeat from * to * one more time, sl st in first dc. (56)
Rnd 10: Ch2, *dc27, 2dc in next*, repeat from * to * one more time, sl st in first dc. (58)
Rnd 11: Ch2, *dc28, 2dc in next*, repeat from * to * one more time, sl st in first dc. (60)
Rnd 12: Ch2, *dc29, 2dc in next*, repeat from * to * one more time, sl st in first dc. (62)
Rnd 13: Ch2, *dc30, 2dc in next*, repeat from * to * one more time, sl st in first dc. (64)
Rnd 14: Ch2, *dc31, 2dc in next*, repeat from * to * one more time, sl st in first dc. (66)
Rnd 15: Ch2, *dc32, 2dc in next*, repeat from * to * one more time, sl st in first dc. (68)
Rnd 16: Ch2, *dc33, 2dc in next*, repeat from * to * one more time, sl st in first dc. (70)
Rnd 17: Ch2, *dc34, 2dc in next*, repeat from * to * one more time, sl st in first dc. (72)
Rnd 18: Ch2, *dc35, 2dc in next*, repeat from * to * one more time, sl st in first dc. (74)
Rnd 19: Ch2, *dc36, 2dc in next*, repeat from * to * one more time, sl st in first dc. (76)
Rnd 20: Ch2, *dc37, 2dc in next*, repeat from * to * one more time, sl st in first dc. (78)
Cut a long tail to close body and attach feet in the end.

FEET (MAKE 2)

Rnd 1: Start with a magic ring, 6sc in the loop. (6)
Rnd 2: 2sc in each stitch around. (12)
Rnd 3: *Sc1, 2sc in next*, repeat from * to * around. (18)
Rnd 4: *Sc2, 2sc in next*, repeat from * to * around. (24)
Rnd 5–Rnd 11: Sc1 in each stitch around. (24)
Rnd 12: *Sc1, (in next: hdc1, dc1, tr1, dc1, hdc1), sc1, sl st 1*, repeat from * to * around. You'll end up with three toes (6 repeats).
Cut a long tail to close the seam of the feet in the end.

TAIL

Rnd 1: Start with a magic ring, ch2 (doesn't count as first stitch from now on), 12dc in the loop, sl st in first dc. (12)
Rnd 2: Ch2, 2dc in each stitch around, sl st in first dc. (24)
Rnd 3: Ch2, dc5, 5dc in next, dc8, 5dc in next, dc8, 5dc in next, sl st in first dc. (36)
Rnd 4: Ch2, dc7, 5dc in next, dc12, 5dc in next, dc12, 5dc in next, dc2, sl st in first dc. (48)
Rnd 5: Ch2, dc9, 5dc in next, dc16, 5dc in next, dc16, 5dc in next, dc4, sl st in first dc. (60)
Rnd 6: Ch2, dc11, 3sc in next, *sc1, (in next: hdc1, dc1, tr1, dc1, hdc1), sc1, sl st 1*, repeat from * to * 4 more times, (in next: hdc1, dc1, tr1, dc1, hdc1), *sl st 1, sc1, (in next: hdc1, dc1, tr1, dc1, hdc1), sc1*, repeat from * to * 4 more times, 3sc in next, dc6, sl st in first dc.
Cut a long tail to close and attach to body in the end.

ARMS (MAKE 2)

Rnd 1: Start with a magic ring, 6sc in the loop. (6)
Rnd 2: 2sc in each stitch around. (12)
Rnd 3: *Sc1, 2sc in next*, repeat from * to * around. (18)
Rnd 4: *Sc2, 2sc in next*, repeat from * to * around. (24)
Rnd 5–Rnd 9: Sc1 in each stitch around. (24)
Rnd 10: *Sc2, sc2tog*, repeat from * to * around. (18)
Rnd 11–Rnd 12: Sc1 in each stitch around. (18)
Rnd 13: Sl st 1, ch2, dc1 in each stitch around, sl st in first dc. (18)
Rnd 14: Ch2, dc1 in each stitch around, sl st in first dc. (18)
At this point, stuff the hand (not too much) and sew across the arm between Rnd 12 and Rnd 13.
Rnd 15–Rnd 17: Ch2, dc1 in each stitch around, sl st in first dc. (18)
Rnd 18: Ch2, *dc1, dc2tog*, repeat from * to * around, sl st in first dc. (12)
Rnd 19–Rnd 22: Ch2, dc1 in each stitch around, sl st in first dc. (12)
Cut a long tail to attach arms to body in the end.

PUTTING IT ALL TOGETHER

- Place each foot between the bottom two layers of the body; use the remaining yarn from the body and sew across the seam, with the feet in between, to close and at the same time attach the feet.
- Stuff the feet lightly. With the remaining yarn sew each foot closed, going through both layers of toes.
- Fold the tail in half so the spikes are lined up; sew closed. Sew the tail to the body.
- Sew the head to the top of the body.
- Finally, sew an arm to each side of the body.

BABY CROCODILE

This freshly hatched baby croc needs a hug.

DIMENSIONS

7.1 in. (18 cm) long and 3.9 in. (10 cm) wide

MATERIALS

DK #3 lightweight yarn (sample shown in Scheepjes Stone Washed):
- green (819 New Jade): 142.2 yd. (130 m)

Crochet hook: US D-3 (3 mm)
Black safety eyes, 10 mm
Fiberfill stuffing
Yarn needle and scissors

DIFFICULTY LEVEL

EYES (MAKE 2)

Rnd 1: Start with a magic ring, 6sc in the loop. (6)
Rnd 2: 2sc in each stitch around. (12)
Rnd 3–Rnd 5: Sc1 in each stitch around. (12)
Cut yarn and weave in ends for the first eye; don't cut yarn for the second eye, but continue with instructions for the head.

HEAD

In the next rounds you'll connect the eyes to make the top of the head.
Rnd 1: Continue with the second eye, sc5, take the first eye and sc2tog in the next stitch of the second and first eyes through both layers. Sc10, sc2tog in the next stitch of the first and second eyes through both layers, sc5. (22)
Rnd 2: *2sc in first stitch, sc10*, repeat from * to * one more time. (24)
Rnd 3: *2sc in each of the next 2 stitches, sc10*, repeat from * to * one more time. (28)
Rnd 4: *2sc in each of the next 4 stitches, sc10*, repeat from * to * one more time. (36)
Rnd 5: Sc1 in each stitch around. (36)
Rnd 6: Sc4, sc2tog, sc16, sc2tog, sc12. (34)
Rnd 7: Sc4, sc2tog, sc15, sc2tog, sc11. (32)
Rnd 8: Sc4, sc2tog, sc14, sc2tog, sc10. (30) Attach safety eyes and center them in between Rnd 5 of the eyes and Rnd 1 of the head.

Rnd 9: Sc4, sc2tog, sc13, sc2tog, sc9. (28)
Rnd 10: Sc4, sc2tog, sc12, sc2tog, sc8. (26)
Rnd 11: Sc4, sc2tog, sc11, sc2tog, sc7. (24)
Rnd 12: Sc4, sc2tog, sc10, sc2tog, sc6. (22)
Rnd 13: Sc4, sc2tog, sc9, sc2tog, sc5. (20)
Rnd 14: Sc4, sc2tog, sc8, sc2tog, sc4. (18) Stuff the head.
Rnd 15: 4dc in next, sc3, 4dc in next, sc2, sl st1, sc2, 4dc in next, sc3, 4dc in next, sc1, sl st1. This round ends here. Cut a long tail, stuff the head more if needed, and sew the mouth shut.

BODY

Rnd 1: Ch13, 1dc in third ch from hook, dc9, 3dc in last, continue along other side of chains, dc10, 3dc in last, sl st in first dc. (26)
Rnd 2: Ch2 (doesn't count as first stitch now and throughout), *dc12, 2dc in next*, repeat from * to * one more time, sl st in first dc. (28)
Rnd 3: Ch2, *dc13, 2dc in next*, repeat from * to * one more time, sl st in first dc. (30)
Rnd 4: Ch2, *dc14, 2dc in next*, repeat from * to * one more time, sl st in first dc. (32)
Rnd 5: Ch2, *dc15, 2dc in next*, repeat from * to * one more time, sl st in first dc. (34)
Rnd 6: Ch2, *dc16, 2dc in next*, repeat from * to * one more time, sl st in first dc. (36)
Rnd 7: Ch2, *dc17, 2dc in next*, repeat from * to * one more time, sl st in first dc. (38)
Rnd 8: Ch2, *dc18, 2dc in next*, repeat from * to * one more time, sl st in first dc. (40)
Rnd 9: Ch2, *dc19, 2dc in next*, repeat from * to * one more time, sl st in first dc. (42)
Rnd 10: Ch2, *dc20, 2dc in next*, repeat from * to * one more time, sl st in first dc. (44)
Rnd 11: Ch2, *dc21, 2dc in next*, repeat from * to * one more time, sl st in first dc. (46)
Rnd 12: Ch2, *dc22, 2dc in next*, repeat from * to * one more time, sl st in first dc. (48) Cut a long tail to close the body later.

ARMS (MAKE 2)

Rnd 1: Start with a magic ring, 6sc in the loop. (6)
Rnd 2: 2sc in each stitch around. (12)
Rnd 3: *Sc1, 2sc in next*, repeat from * to * around. (18)
Rnd 4–Rnd 5: Sc1 in each stitch around. (18)
Rnd 6: *Sc1, sc2tog*, repeat from * to * around. (12)
Rnd 7: Sc1 in each stitch around. (12)
Rnd 8: Sl st 1, ch2 (doesn't count as first stitch now and throughout), dc1 in each stitch around, sl st in first dc. (12)
Rnd 9: Ch2, dc2tog, dc1 in each stitch around, sl st in first dc. (11)
At this point, stuff the hand. Use a small piece of yarn and sew across the arm between Rnd 7 and Rnd 8.
Rnd 10: Ch2, dc1 in each stitch around, sl st in first dc. (11)
Rnd 11: Ch2, dc2tog, dc1 in each stitch around, sl st in first dc. (10)
Rnd 12: Ch2, dc1 in each stitch around, sl st in first dc. (10)
Cut a long tail to sew an arm to each side of the body between Rnd 1 and Rnd 3.

FEET (MAKE 2)

Rnd 1: Start with a magic ring, 6sc in the loop. (6)
Rnd 2: 2sc in each stitch around. (12)
Rnd 3: *Sc1, 2sc in next*, repeat from * to * around. (18)
Rnd 4–Rnd 5: Sc1 in each stitch around. (18)
Rnd 6: *Sc1, (in next: hdc1, dc1, tr1, dc1, hdc1), sl st 1*, repeat from * to * around. You'll end up with three toes (6 repeats).
Cut a long tail to close the feet at the end.

TAIL

Rnd 1: Start with a magic ring, ch2 (doesn't count as first dc for entire tail), dc12 in the loop, sl st in first dc. (12)
Rnd 2: Ch2, dc1, 5dc in next, dc4, 5dc in next, dc4, 5dc in next, sl st in first dc. (24)
Rnd 3: Ch2, dc3, 5dc in next, dc8, 5dc in next, dc8, 5dc in next, dc2, sl st in first dc. (36)
Rnd 4: Ch1 (doesn't count as first sc), sc5, 3sc in next, *sc1, 4dc in next, sc1*, repeat from * to * 3 more times, 3sc in next, *sc1, 4dc in next, sc1*, repeat from * to * 3 more times, 3sc in next, sc4, sl st in first sc. (72; you'll have one straight side and two sides with a pointy edging)
Cut a long tail to close the tail and sew it to the body at the end.

PUTTING IT ALL TOGETHER

- Place the feet in between the two layers of the body at the bottom. With the remaining yarn of the body, sew along the bottom to close the body and attach the feet at the same time.
- Stuff the feet lightly. With the remaining yarn, close each foot through both layers of the toes.
- Sew Rnd 5 of the head (eyes not included) to Rnd 1 of the body.
- Sew an arm to each side of the body in Rnds 1–3.
- Finally, fold the tail so the pointy edging is aligned and sew closed. Sew to one side of the body in the bottom 3 rounds.

DOG

This dog will be your loyal companion.

DIMENSIONS

12.2 in. (31 cm) long and 6.3 in. (16 cm) wide

MATERIALS

DK #3 lightweight yarn (sample shown in Scheepjes Stone Washed):
• ochre yellow (Yellow Jasper): 284.3 yd. (260 m)
Crochet hook: US size D-3 (3 mm)
Black and blue safety eyes, 15 mm
Black or brown safety nose, 15 mm
Fiberfill stuffing
Yarn needle and scissors

DIFFICULTY LEVEL

EYELIDS (MAKE 2)

Rnd 1: Start with a magic ring. 6sc in the ring. (6) When pulling the magic ring, put your hook inside to make sure you have enough room to put the safety eyes in later.
Rnd 2: Sl st 1, ch2 (doesn't count as first dc), dc4, ch1, sl st 1 in next. Cut yarn and weave in ends.

HEAD

Rnd 1: Start with a magic ring, 6sc in the ring. (6)
Rnd 2: 2sc in each stitch around. (12)
Rnd 3: *Sc1, 2sc in next*, repeat from * to * around. (18)
Rnd 4: *Sc2, 2sc in next*, repeat from * to * around. (24)
Rnd 5: *Sc3, 2sc in next*, repeat from * to * around. (30)
Rnd 6: *Sc4, 2sc in next*, repeat from * to * around. (36)
Rnd 7: *Sc5, 2sc in next*, repeat from * to * around. (42)
Rnd 8: *Sc6, 2sc in next*, repeat from * to * around. (48)
Rnd 9–Rnd 15: Sc1 in each stitch around. (48)
Rnd 16: 3sc in next, sc1, 3sc in next, sc45. (52)
Rnd 17: Sc1, 3sc in next, sc3, 3sc in next, sc46. (56)
Rnd 18: Sc2, 3sc in next, sc5, 3sc in next, sc47. (60)
Rnd 19: Sc3, 3sc in next, sc7, 3sc in next, sc48. (64)
Rnd 20–Rnd 24: Sc1 in each stitch around. (64)
Rnd 25: Sc7, sc5tog, sc52. (60)
Rnd 26: *Sc8, sc2tog*, repeat from * to * around. (54)
Rnd 27: *Sc7, sc2tog*, repeat from * to * around. (48)
Rnd 28: *Sc6, sc2tog*, repeat from * to * around. (42)
Rnd 29: *Sc5, sc2tog*, repeat from * to * around. (36)
Put a safety eye inside each eyelid. The eyelids will be folded over the top of the eyes. I recommend stuffing the head lightly to decide the placing of the eyes and nose. Now attach the eyes between Rnd 15 and Rnd 16 on each side of the snout (with 7 stitches in between) and make sure they are really secure, for safety reasons, since it is a little bit harder to attach them with two layers between the eye and the back.
Attach the safety nose between Rnd 21 and Rnd 22 in the center of the snout.

Rnd 30: *Sc4, sc2tog*, repeat from * to * around. (30)
Rnd 31: *Sc3, sc2tog*, repeat from * to * around. (24)
Rnd 32: *Sc2, sc2tog*, repeat from * to * around. (18)
Stuff the head; make sure to stuff the snout to shape it.
Rnd 33: *Sc1, sc2tog*, repeat from * to * around. (12)
Cut yarn, weave through the twelve remaining stitches, pull tight, and secure, leaving a long tail to attach it to the body later.

EARS (MAKE 2)

Rnd 1: Start with a magic ring, ch2 (doesn't count as first dc), dc12 in the loop, sl st in first dc. (12)
Rnd 2: Ch2, 2dc in each stitch around, sl st in first dc. (24)
Rnd 3–Rnd 4: Ch2, dc1 in each stitch around, sl st in first dc. (24)
Rnd 5: Ch2, *dc1, dc2tog*, repeat from * to * around, sl st in first dc. (16)
Rnd 6: Ch2, *dc6, dc2tog*, repeat from * to * around, sl st in first dc. (14)
Rnd 7: Ch2, *dc5, dc2tog *, repeat from * to * around, sl st in first dc. (12)
Rnd 8: Ch2, *dc4, dc2tog *, repeat from * to * around, sl st in first dc. (10)
Rnd 9: Ch2, *dc3, dc2tog *, repeat from * to * around, sl st in first dc. (8)
Rnd 10: Ch2, *dc2, dc2tog *, repeat from * to * around, sl st in first dc. (6) Cut a long tail to attach ears to head later.

BODY

Rnd 1: Ch18, 1dc in third ch from hook, dc14, 3dc in last, continue along other side of chains, dc15, 3dc in last, sl st in first dc. (36)
Rnd 2: Ch2 (doesn't count as first stitch now and throughout), *dc17, 2dc in next*, repeat from * to * one more time, sl st in first dc. (38)
Rnd 3: Ch2, *dc18, 2dc in next*, repeat from * to * one more time, sl st in first dc. (40)
Rnd 4: Ch2, *dc19, 2dc in next*, repeat from * to * one more time, sl st in first dc. (42)
Rnd 5: Ch2, *dc20, 2dc in next*, repeat from * to * one more time, sl st in first dc. (44)
Rnd 6: Ch2, *dc21, 2dc in next*, repeat from * to * one more time, sl st in first dc. (46)
Rnd 7: Ch2, *dc22, 2dc in next*, repeat from * to * one more time, sl st in first dc. (48)
Rnd 8: Ch2, *dc23, 2dc in next*, repeat from * to * one more time, sl st in first dc. (50)
Rnd 9: Ch2, *dc24, 2dc in next*, repeat from * to * one more time, sl st in first dc. (52)
Rnd 10: Ch2, *dc25, 2dc in next*, repeat from * to * one more time, sl st in first dc. (54)
Rnd 11: Ch2, *dc26, 2dc in next*, repeat from * to * one more time, sl st in first dc. (56)
Rnd 12: Ch2, *dc27, 2dc in next*, repeat from * to * one more time, sl st in first dc. (58)
Rnd 13: Ch2, *dc28, 2dc in next*, repeat from * to * one more time, sl st in first dc. (60)
Rnd 14: Ch2, *dc29, 2dc in next*, repeat from * to * one more time, sl st in first dc. (62)
Rnd 15: Ch2, *dc30, 2dc in next*, repeat from * to * one more time, sl st in first dc. (64)
Rnd 16: Ch2, *dc31, 2dc in next*, repeat from * to * one more time, sl st in first dc. (66)
Rnd 17: Ch2, *dc32, 2dc in next*, repeat from * to * one more time, sl st in first dc. (68)
Rnd 18: Ch2, *dc33, 2dc in next*, repeat from * to * one more time, sl st in first dc. (70)
Rnd 19: Ch2, *dc34, 2dc in next*, repeat from * to * one more time, sl st in first dc. (72)
Rnd 20: Ch2, *dc35, 2dc in next*, repeat from * to * one more time, sl st in first dc. (74)
Cut a long tail to close the body; fold the body in line with the increases to make the belly straight.

LEGS (MAKE 2)

Rnd 1: Start with a magic ring, ch2 (doesn't count as first dc), dc12 in the loop, sl st in first dc. (12)
Rnd 2: Ch2, *dc1, 2dc in next*, repeat from * to * around, sl st in first dc. (18)
Rnd 3–Rnd 7: Ch2, dc1 in each stitch around, sl st in first dc. (18) Cut yarn and weave in ends.

TAIL

Rnd 1: Start with a magic ring, ch2 (doesn't count as first dc), dc12 in the loop, sl st in first dc. (12)
Rnd 2–Rnd 4: Ch2, dc1 in each stitch around, sl st in first dc. (12)
Cut yarn and weave in ends.

ARMS (MAKE 2)

Rnd 1: Start with a magic ring, 6sc in the loop. (6)
Rnd 2: 2sc in each stitch around. (12)
Rnd 3: *Sc1, 2sc in next*, repeat from * to * around. (18)
Rnd 4: *Sc2, 2sc in next*, repeat from * to * around. (24)
Rnd 5–Rnd 9: Sc1 in each stitch around. (24)
Rnd 10: *Sc2, sc2tog*, repeat from * to * around. (18)
Rnd 11–Rnd 12: Sc1 in each stitch around. (18)
Rnd 13: Sl st 1, ch2 (doesn't count as first stitch now and throughout), dc1 in each stitch around, sl st in first dc. (18)
Rnd 14: Ch2, dc2tog, dc1 in each stitch around, sl st in first dc. (17)
At this point, stuff the hand. Take a small piece of the yarn and sew across the arm between Rnd 12 and Rnd 13.
Rnd 15: Ch2, dc1 in each stitch around, sl st in first dc. (17)
Rnd 16: Ch2, dc2tog, dc1 in each stitch around, sl st in first dc. (16)

Rnd 17: Ch2, dc1 in each stitch around, sl st in first dc. (16)
Rnd 18: Ch2, dc2tog, dc1 in each stitch around, sl st in first dc. (15)
Rnd 19: Ch2, dc1 in each stitch around, sl st in first dc. (15)
Rnd 20: Ch2, dc2tog, dc1 in each stitch around, sl st in first dc. (14)
Rnd 21: Ch2, dc1 in each stitch around, sl st in first dc. (14)
Rnd 22: Ch2, dc2tog, dc1 in each stitch around, sl st in first dc. (13)
Cut a long tail to attach arms to body later.

PUTTING IT ALL TOGETHER

- Sew ears to each side of the head in Rnd 10.
- Place both legs and the tail between the bottom two layers of the body. With the remaining yarn from the body, sew across the seam with the parts in between. This way you close the bottom and assemble the pieces at the same time.
- Sew an arm to each side of the body between Rnd 1 and Rnd 3.
- Finally, sew Rnd 27 of the head to Rnd 1 of the body.

PUPPY

DIMENSIONS

6.3 in (16 cm) long and 3.9 in (10 cm) wide

MATERIALS

DK #3 lightweight yarn (sample shown in Scheepjes Stone Washed):
- brown (Brown Agate): 142.2 yd. (130 m)

Crochet hook: US size D-3 (3 mm)
Black and blue safety eyes, 15 mm
Black or brown safety nose, 15 mm
Fiberfill stuffing
Yarn needle and scissors

DIFFICULTY LEVEL

EYELIDS (MAKE 2)

Rnd 1: Start with a magic ring, 6sc in the ring. (6) When pulling the magic ring, put your hook inside to make sure you have enough room to put the safety eye in later.
Rnd 2: *Sc1, 2sc in next*, repeat from * to * one more time, sl st 1 to finish. Cut yarn and weave in ends.

HEAD

Rnd 1: Start with a magic ring, 6sc in the ring. (6)
Rnd 2: 2sc in each stitch around. (12)
Rnd 3: *Sc1, 2sc in next*, repeat from * to * around. (18)
Rnd 4: *Sc2, 2sc in next*, repeat from * to * around. (24)
Rnd 5: *Sc3, 2sc in next*, repeat from * to * around. (30)
Rnd 6: *Sc4, 2sc in next*, repeat from * to * around. (36)
Rnd 7–Rnd 11: Sc1 in each stitch around. (36)
Rnd 12: 2sc in each of the next 5 stitches (this will be the snout), sc31. (41)
Rnd 13–Rnd 16: Sc1 in each stitch around. (41)
Rnd 17: Sc2tog 5 times, sc31. (36)
Rnd 18: *Sc4, sc2tog*, repeat from * to * around. (30)
Rnd 19: *Sc3, sc2tog*, repeat from * to * around. (24)
Rnd 20: *Sc2, sc2tog*, repeat from * to * around. (18)
Put a safety eye inside each eyelid; the eyelids will be folded over the top of the eyes. Now attach the eyes between Rnd 10 and Rnd 11 on each side of the snout and make sure they are really secure, for safety reasons, since it is a little bit harder to attach them with two layers between the eye and the back.
Attach the safety nose between Rnd 13 and Rnd 14 in the center of the snout and stuff the head; make sure to stuff the snout to shape it.
Rnd 21: *Sc1, sc2tog*, repeat from * to * around. (12) Cut yarn, weave through the twelve remaining stitches, pull tight, and secure, but leave a long tail to attach it to the body later.

EARS (MAKE 2)

Rnd 1: Start with a magic ring, 6sc in the ring. (6)
Rnd 2: 2sc in each stitch around. (12)
Rnd 3–Rnd 4: Sc1 in each stitch around. (12)
Rnd 5: *Sc1, sc2tog*, repeat from * to * around. (8)
Rnd 6–Rnd 9: Sc1 in each stitch around. (8) Cut yarn but leave a long tail to attach ears to head later.

BODY

Rnd 1: Ch13, 1dc in third ch from hook, dc9, 3dc in last, continue along other side of chains, dc9, 4dc in last, sl st in first dc. (26)
Rnd 2: Ch2 (doesn't count as first stitch now and throughout), *dc12, 2dc in next*, repeat from * to * one more time, sl st in first dc. (28)
Rnd 3: Ch2, *dc13, 2dc in next*, repeat from * to * one more time, sl st in first dc. (30)
Rnd 4: Ch2, *dc14, 2dc in next*, repeat from * to * one more time, sl st in first dc. (32)
Rnd 5: Ch2, *dc15, 2dc in next*, repeat from * to * one more time, sl st in first dc. (34)
Rnd 6: Ch2, *dc16, 2dc in next*, repeat from * to * one more time, sl st in first dc. (36)

Rnd 7: Ch2, *dc17, 2dc in next*, repeat from * to * one more time, sl st in first dc. (38)
Rnd 8: Ch2, *dc18, 2dc in next*, repeat from * to * one more time, sl st in first dc. (40)
Rnd 9: Ch2, *dc19, 2dc in next*, repeat from * to * one more time, sl st in first dc. (42)
Rnd 10: Ch2, *dc20, 2dc in next*, repeat from * to * one more time, sl st in first dc. (44)
Rnd 11: Ch2, *dc21, 2dc in next*, repeat from * to * one more time, sl st in first dc. (46)
Rnd 12: Ch2, *dc22, ch14, 1dc in third ch from hook, 1dc in each of the 11 remaining chains, 2dc in next stitch of Rnd 11*, repeat from * to * one more time, sl st in first dc. Cut a long tail to close the body.

ARMS (MAKE 2)

Rnd 1: Start with a magic ring, 6sc in the loop. (6)
Rnd 2: 2sc in each stitch around. (12)
Rnd 3: *Sc1, 2sc in next*, repeat from * to * around. (18)
Rnd 4–Rnd 5: Sc1 in each stitch around. (18)
Rnd 6: *Sc1, sc2tog*, repeat from * to * around. (12)
Rnd 7: Sc1 in each stitch around. (12)
Rnd 8: Sl st 1, ch2 (doesn't count as first stitch now and throughout), dc1 in each stitch around, sl st in first dc. (12)
Rnd 9: Ch2, dc2tog, dc1 in each stitch around, sl st in first dc. (11)
At this point, stuff the hand, take a small piece of the brown yarn, and sew across the arm between Rnd 7 and Rnd 8.
Rnd 10: Ch2, dc1 in each stitch around, sl st in first dc. (11)
Rnd 11: Ch2, dc2tog, dc1 in each stitch around, sl st in first dc. (10)
Rnd 12: Ch2, dc1 in each stitch around, sl st in first dc. (10)
Rnd 13: Ch2, dc2tog, dc1 in each stitch around, sl st in first dc. (9)
Cut a long tail to attach arms to body later.

PUTTING IT ALL TOGETHER

- Sew an ear on either side of the head at Rnd 6.
- Fold the body along the increase lines to make the belly straight and sew it closed. Tie a knot in the corners to form the feet.
- Sew an arm on either side of the body between Rnd 1 and Rnd 2.
- Sew Rnd 18 of the head to Rnd 1 of the body.

FOX

You will want to cuddle this very soft fox.

DIMENSIONS

10.6 in. (27 cm) long and 6.3 in. (16 cm) wide

MATERIALS

DK #3 lightweight yarn (sample shown in Scheepjes Stone Washed):
- orange (Coral): 142.2 yd. (130 m)
- white (Moon Stone): 76.6 yd. (70 m)
- black (Black Onyx): 76.6 yd. (70 m)

Crochet hook: US size D-3 (3 mm)
Black and gold safety eyes, 15 mm
Fiberfill stuffing
Yarn needle and scissors

DIFFICULTY LEVEL

HEAD

Rnd 1: With black, start with a magic ring, 6sc in the loop. (6)
Rnd 2: *Sc1, 2sc in next*, repeat from * to * around. (9)
Rnd 3: With white *Sc2, 2sc in next*, repeat from * to * around. (12)
Rnd 4: *Sc3, 2sc in next*, repeat from * to * around. (15)
Rnd 5: *Sc4, 2sc in next*, repeat from * to * around. (18)
Rnd 6: *Sc5, 2sc in next*, repeat from * to * around. (21)
Rnd 7: *Sc6, 2sc in next*, repeat from * to * around. (24)
Rnd 8: With orange *sc3, 2sc in next*, repeat from * to * around. (30)
Rnd 9: *Sc4, 2sc in next*, repeat from * to * around. (36)
Rnd 10: *Sc5, 2sc in next*, repeat from * to * around. (42)
Rnd 11: *Sc6, 2sc in next*, repeat from * to * around. (48)
Rnd 12–Rnd 21: Sc1 in each stitch around. (48)
Attach a safety eye between Rnd 12 and Rnd 13, on either side of the snout; make sure the first stitch (where you can see the color change) is on the back.
Rnd 22: *Sc6, sc2tog*, repeat from * to * around. (42)
Rnd 23: *Sc5, sc2tog*, repeat from * to * around. (36)
Rnd 24: *Sc4, sc2tog*, repeat from * to * around. (30)
Rnd 25: *Sc3, sc2tog*, repeat from * to * around. (24)
Rnd 26: *Sc2, sc2tog*, repeat from * to * around. (18)
Stuff the head.
Rnd 27: *Sc1, sc2tog*, repeat from * to * around. (12)
Cut a long thread, weave through the front loops of the remaining stitches, pull tight, secure, and weave in ends.

EARS (MAKE 2)

Rnd 1: With black, start with a magic ring, 6sc in the loop. (6)
Rnd 2: *Sc1, 2sc in next*, repeat from * to * around. (9)
Rnd 3: *Sc2, 2sc in next*, repeat from * to * around. (12)
Rnd 4: With orange *sc3, 2sc in next*, repeat from * to * around. (15)
Rnd 5: *Sc4, 2sc in next*, repeat from * to * around. (18)
Rnd 6: *Sc5, 2sc in next*, repeat from * to * around. (21)
Rnd 7–Rnd 10: Sc1 in each stitch around. (21)
Cut the yarn but leave a long tail to attach the ears in the end.

BODY

Rnd 1: With orange ch18, 1dc in third ch from hook, dc14, 3dc in last, continue along other side of chains, dc15, 3dc in last, sl st in first dc. (36)

Rnd 2: Ch2 (doesn't count as first stitch now and throughout), *dc17, 2dc in next*, repeat from * to * one more time, sl st in first dc. (38)
Rnd 3: Ch2, *dc18, 2dc in next*, repeat from * to * one more time, sl st in first dc. (40)
Rnd 4: Ch2, *dc19, 2dc in next*, repeat from * to * one more time, sl st in first dc. (42)
Rnd 5: Ch2, *dc20, 2dc in next*, repeat from * to * one more time, sl st in first dc. (44)
Rnd 6: Ch2, *dc21, 2dc in next*, repeat from * to * one more time, sl st in first dc. (46)
Rnd 7: Ch2, *dc22, 2dc in next*, repeat from * to * one more time, sl st in first dc. (48)
Rnd 8: Ch2, *dc23, 2dc in next*, repeat from * to * one more time, sl st in first dc. (50)
Rnd 9: Ch2, *dc24, 2dc in next*, repeat from * to * one more time, sl st in first dc. (52)
Rnd 10: Ch2, *dc25, 2dc in next*, repeat from * to * one more time, sl st in first dc. (54)
Rnd 11: Ch2, *dc26, 2dc in next*, repeat from * to * one more time, sl st in first dc. (56)
Rnd 12: Ch2, *dc27, 2dc in next*, repeat from * to * one more time, sl st in first dc. (58)
Rnd 13: Ch2, *dc28, 2dc in next*, repeat from * to * one more time, sl st in first dc. (60)
Rnd 14: Ch2, *dc29, 2dc in next*, repeat from * to * one more time, sl st in first dc. (62)
Rnd 15: Ch2, *dc30, 2dc in next*, repeat from * to * one more time, sl st in first dc. (64)
Rnd 16: Ch2, *dc31, 2dc in next*, repeat from * to * one more time, sl st in first dc. (66)
Rnd 17: Ch2, *dc32, 2dc in next*, repeat from * to * one more time, sl st in first dc. (68)
Rnd 18: Ch2, *dc33, 2dc in next*, repeat from * to * one more time, sl st in first dc. (70)
Rnd 19: Ch2, *dc34, 2dc in next*, repeat from * to * one more time, sl st in first dc. (72)
Cut a long tail to close the body; fold the body in line with the increases to make the belly straight.

ARMS (MAKE 2)

Rnd 1: With black, start with a magic ring, 6sc in the loop. (6)
Rnd 2: 2sc in each stitch around. (12)
Rnd 3: *Sc1, 2sc in next*, repeat from * to * around. (18)
Rnd 4: *Sc2, 2sc in next*, repeat from * to * around. (24)
Rnd 5–Rnd 9: Sc1 in each stitch around. (24)
Rnd 10: *Sc2, sc2tog*, repeat from * to * around. (18)
Rnd 11–Rnd 12: Sc1 in each stitch around. (18)
Cut a long thread; you'll use it after Rnd 14.
Rnd 13: With orange sl st 1, ch2 (doesn't count as first stitch now and throughout), dc1 in each stitch around, sl st in first dc. (18)
Rnd 14: Ch2, dc2tog, dc1 in each stitch around, sl st in first dc. (17)
At this point, stuff the hand. Take the remaining black yarn and sew across the arm between Rnd 12 and Rnd 13.
Rnd 15: Ch2, dc1 in each stitch around, sl st in first dc. (17)
Rnd 16: Ch2, dc2tog, dc1 in each stitch around, sl st in first dc. (16)
Rnd 17: Ch2, dc1 in each stitch around, sl st in first dc. (16)
Rnd 18: Ch2, dc2tog, dc1 in each stitch around, sl st in first dc. (15)
Rnd 19: Ch2, dc1 in each stitch around, sl st in first dc. (15)
Rnd 20: Ch2, dc2tog, dc1 in each stitch around, sl st in first dc. (14)
Rnd 21: Ch2, dc1 in each stitch around, sl st in first dc. (14)
Rnd 22: Ch2, dc2tog, dc1 in each stitch around, sl st in first dc. (13)
Cut a long tail to attach arms to body later.

LEGS (MAKE 2)

Rnd 1: With black, start with a magic ring, ch2 (doesn't count as first dc), 12dc in the loop, sl st in first dc. (12)
Rnd 2: Ch2, *dc1, 2dc in next*, repeat from * to * around, sl st in first dc. (18)
Rnd 3–Rnd 4: Ch2, dc1 in each stitch around, sl st in first dc. (18)
Rnd 5–Rnd 6: With orange ch2, dc1 in each stitch around, sl st in first dc. (18)
Cut yarn and weave in ends.

TAIL

Rnd 1: With white, start with a magic ring, ch2 (doesn't count as first dc), 6dc in the loop, sl st in first dc. (6)
Rnd 2: Ch2, *dc1, 2dc in next*, repeat from * to * around, sl st in first dc. (9)
Rnd 3: Ch2, *dc2, 2dc in next*, repeat from * to * around, sl st in first dc. (12)
Rnd 4: Ch2, *dc3, 2dc in next*, repeat from * to * around, sl st in first dc. (15)
Rnd 5: With orange ch2, *dc2, 2dc in next*, repeat from * to * around, sl st in first dc. (20)
Rnd 6: Ch2, *dc3, 2dc in next*, repeat from * to * around, sl st in first dc. (25)
Rnd 7: Ch2, *dc4, 2dc in next*, repeat from * to * around, sl st in first dc. (30)
Rnd 8–Rnd 9: Ch2, dc1 in each stitch around, sl st in first dc. (30)
Rnd 10: Ch2, *dc3, dc2tog*, repeat from * to * around, sl st in first dc. (24)
Rnd 11: Ch2, *dc2, dc2tog*, repeat from * to * around, sl st in first dc. (18)
Rnd 12: Ch2, *dc1, dc2tog*, repeat from * to * around, sl st in first dc. (12)
Cut a long tail to attach tail to body later.

PUTTING IT ALL TOGETHER

- Place the legs between the bottom two layers of the body. With the remaining yarn from the body, sew across the seam with the legs in between. This way you close the bottom and assemble the pieces at the same time.
- Sew the tail to the body against the bottom 3 rounds.
- Sew an arm to each side of the body between Rnd 1 and Rnd 3.
- Use pins to determine the placement of the ears. For example, attach them with a slight rounding, one corner from Rnd 22 and the other corner from Rnd 17; in Rnd 22 they are 6 stitches apart. Sew the ears in place.
- Finally, sew Rnd 16 of the head to Rnd 1 of the body.

You will never want to let go of this little fox!

DIMENSIONS

5.9 in. (15 cm) long and 3.9 in. (10 cm) wide

MATERIALS

DK #3 lightweight yarn (sample shown in Scheepjes Stone Washed):
- orange (Coral): 120.3 yd. (110 m)
- white (Moon Stone): 32.8 yd. (30 m)
- black (Black Onyx): 54.7 yd. (50 m)

Crochet hook: US size D-3 (3 mm)
Black with gold safety eyes, 12 mm
Fiberfill stuffing
Yarn needle and scissors

DIFFICULTY LEVEL

HEAD

Rnd 1: With black, start with a magic ring, 6sc in the loop. (6)
Rnd 2: *Sc1, 2sc in next*, repeat from * to * around. (9)
Rnd 3: With white *sc2, 2sc in next*, repeat from * to * around. (12)
Rnd 4: *Sc3, 2sc in next*, repeat from * to * around. (15)
Rnd 5: *Sc4, 2sc in next*, repeat from * to * around. (18)
Rnd 6: With orange *sc2, 2sc in next*, repeat from * to * around. (24)
Rnd 7: *Sc3, 2sc in next*, repeat from * to * around. (30)
Rnd 8: *Sc4, 2sc in next*, repeat from * to * around. (36)
Rnd 9–Rnd 16: Sc1 in each stitch around. (36)
Attach the safety eyes between Rnd 8 and Rnd 9, on both sides of the snout, but make sure that the first stitch (where you can see the color change) is on the back.
Rnd 17: *Sc4, sc2tog*, repeat from * to * around. (30)
Rnd 18: *Sc3, sc2tog*, repeat from * to * around. (24)
Rnd 19: *Sc2, sc2tog*, repeat from * to * around. (18)
Stuff the head.
Rnd 20: *Sc1, sc2tog*, repeat from * to * around. (12)
Cut a long thread, weave through the front loops of the remaining stitches, pull tight, secure and weave in ends.

EARS (MAKE 2)

Rnd 1: With black, start with a magic ring, 6sc in the loop. (6)
Rnd 2: *Sc1, 2sc in next*, repeat from * to * around. (9)
Rnd 3: *Sc2, 2sc in next*, repeat from * to * around. (12)
Rnd 4: With orange *sc3, 2sc in next*, repeat from * to * around. (15)
Rnd 5–Rnd 7: Sc1 in each stitch around. (15)
Cut the yarn but leave a long tail to attach the ears in the end.

BODY

Rnd 1: With orange ch13, dc1 in 3rd ch from hook, dc9, 3dc in last, continue along other side of chains, dc10, 3dc in last, sl st in first dc. (26)
Rnd 2: Ch2 (doesn't count as first stitch now and throughout), *dc12, 2dc in next* repeat from * to * one more time, sl st in first dc. (28)
Rnd 3: Ch2, *dc13, 2dc in next*, repeat from * to * one more time, sl st in first dc. (30)
Rnd 4: Ch2, *dc14, 2dc in next*, repeat from * to * one more time, sl st in first dc. (32)
Rnd 5: Ch2, *dc15, 2dc in next*, repeat from * to * one more time, sl st in first dc. (34)
Rnd 6: Ch2, *dc16, 2dc in next*, repeat from * to * one more time, sl st in first dc. (36)
Rnd 7: Ch2, *dc17, 2dc in next*, repeat from * to * one more time, sl st in first dc. (38)
Rnd 8: Ch2, *dc18, 2dc in next*, repeat from * to * one more time, sl st in first dc. (40)
Rnd 9: Ch2, *dc19, 2dc in next*, repeat from * to * one more time, sl st in first dc. (42)
Rnd 10: Ch2, *dc20, 2dc in next*, repeat from * to * one more time, sl st in first dc. (44)
Rnd 11: Ch2, *dc21, 2dc in next*, repeat from * to * one more time, sl st in first dc. (46)
Rnd 12: Ch2, ***with orange** dc22, **with black** ch14, dc1 in 3rd ch from hook, dc1 in each of the remaining 11 chains, **with orange** 2dc in next stitch of Rnd 11*, repeat from * to * one more time, sl st in first dc. Cut a long tail to close the body later.

ARMS (MAKE 2)

Rnd 1: With black, start with a magic ring, 6sc in the loop. (6)
Rnd 2: 2sc in each stitch around. (12)
Rnd 3: *Sc1, 2sc in next*, repeat from * to * around. (18)
Rnd 4–Rnd 5: Sc1 in each stitch around. (18)
Rnd 6: *Sc1, sc2tog*, repeat from * to * around. (12)
Rnd 7: Sc1 in each stitch around. (12) Cut a long thread; you'll use it after Rnd 9.
Rnd 8: With orange sl st 1, ch2 (doesn't count as first stitch now and throughout), dc1 in each stitch around, sl st in first dc. (12)

Rnd 9: Ch2, dc2tog, dc1 in each stitch around, sl st in first dc. (11)

At this point, stuff the hand. Take the remaining black yarn and sew across the arm between Rnd 7 and Rnd 8.

Rnd 10: Ch2, dc1 in each stitch around, sl st in first dc. (11)

Rnd 11: Ch2, dc2tog, dc1 in each stitch around, sl st in first dc. (10)

Rnd 12: Ch2, dc1 in each stitch around, sl st in first dc. (10)

Rnd 13: Ch2, dc2tog, dc1 in each stitch around, sl st in first dc. (9)

Cut a long tail to attach arms to body later.

TAIL

Rnd 1: With white, start with a magic ring, ch2 (doesn't count as first dc), 6dc in the loop, sl st in first dc. (6)

Rnd 2: Ch2, *dc1, 2dc in next*, repeat from * to * around, sl st in first dc. (9)

Rnd 3: Ch2, *dc2, 2dc in next*, repeat from * to * around, sl st in first dc. (12)

Rnd 4: With orange ch2, *dc1, 2dc in next*, repeat from * to * around, sl st in first dc. (18)

Rnd 5: Ch2, *dc2, 2dc in next*, repeat from * to * around, sl st in first dc. (24)

Rnd 6: Ch2, dc1 in each stitch around, sl st in first dc. (24)

Rnd 7: Ch2, *dc2, dc2tog*, repeat from * to * around, sl st in first dc. (18)

Rnd 8: Ch2, *dc1, dc2tog*, repeat around, sl st in first dc. (12) Cut a long thread to attach tail to body later.

PUTTING IT ALL TOGETHER

- Use pins to determine the placement of the ears. Attach them with a slight rounding, the top corner in Rnd 16 of the head and the other corner in Rnd 12; at the top of the head, in Rnd 16, the ears are 6 stitches apart. Sew the ears in place.
- Fold the body in line with the increases to make the belly straight and sew closed with the remaining yarn. Tie a knot in the corners to form the feet.
- Sew an arm to each side of the body in Rnd 1 and Rnd 2.
- Sew the tail to the body against Rnd 10 to Rnd 12.
- Finally, sew Rnd 13 of the head to Rnd 1 of the body.

FROG

DIMENSIONS

14.2 in. (36 cm) high and 5.9 in. (15 cm) wide

MATERIALS

DK #3 lightweight yarn (sample shown in Scheepjes Stone Washed):

- light green (New Jade): 87.5 yd. (80 m)
- dark green (Canada Jade): 196.9 yd. (180 m)

Crochet hook: US size D-3 (3 mm)

Gold and black safety eyes, 15 mm

Fiberfill stuffing

Needle and scissors

DIFFICULTY LEVEL

EYES (MAKE 2)

Rnd 1: With dark green, start with a magic ring, 6sc in the ring. (6)
Rnd 2: 2sc in each stitch around. (12)
Rnd 3: *Sc1, 2sc in next*, repeat from * to * around. (18)
Rnd 4: *Sc2, 2sc in next*, repeat from * to * around. (24)
Rnd 5–Rnd 8: Sc1 in each stitch around. (24)
For the first eye, tie the thread off; for the second eye, let the thread hang and continue with the head.

HEAD

The eyes are connected and form the top of the head.
Rnd 1: Continue with the second eye, sc11, take the first eye and crochet the next stitch of the second eye and the first eye together, sc22, crochet the next stitch of the first and second eye together, sc11. (46)
Rnd 2: 2sc in first stitch, sc22, 2sc in next stitch, sc22. (48)
Rnd 3: *Sc7, 2sc in next*, repeat from * to * around. (54)
Rnd 4–Rnd 8: Sc1 in each stitch around. (54)
Rnd 9: With dark green sc7, **with light green** sc18, **with dark green** sc29. (54)
Rnd 10: With dark green sc8, **with light green** sc17, **with dark green** sc29. (54)
Rnd 11: With dark green sc9, **with light green** sc16, **with dark green** sc29. (54)
Rnd 12: With dark green sc10, **with light green** sc15, **with dark green** sc29. (54)
Rnd 13: With dark green sc7, sc2tog, sc2, **with light green** sc5, sc2tog, sc5, sc2tog, **with dark green** sc9, *sc2tog, sc7*, repeat from * to * to last 2 stitches, sc2tog. (48)
Rnd 14: With dark green sc6, sc2tog, sc3, **with light green** sc4, sc2tog, sc3, sc2tog, **with dark green** *sc6, sc2tog*, repeat from * to * to last 2 stitches, sc2. (42)
Rnd 15: With dark green sc5, sc2tog, sc4, **with light green** sc1, sc2tog, sc3, sc2tog, **with dark green** sc7, *sc2tog, sc5*, repeat from * to * to last 2 stitches, sc2tog. (36)
Rnd 16: With dark green sc4, sc2tog, sc3, sc2tog, **with light green** sc3, sc2tog, **with dark green** *sc4, sc2tog*, repeat from * to * until last 2 stitches, sc2. (30)
Rnd 17: With dark green sc3, sc2tog, sc3, sc2tog, **with light green** sc3, **with dark green** sc2tog, *sc3, sc2tog*, repeat from * to * to end. (24)
Rnd 18: With dark green sc2, sc2tog, sc2, sc2tog, sc1, **with light green** sc2tog, **with dark green** *sc2, sc2tog*, repeat from * to * to last stitch, sc1. (18) You can cut the light green thread.
At this point, attach the eyes between Rnd 8 of the eye and Rnd 1 of the head and fill the head.
Rnd 19: With dark green *sc1, sc2tog*, repeat from * to * around. (12)
Cut the thread, close the seam with the dark green thread, and neatly hide the light green thread.

BODY

Rnd 1: With dark green ch18, dc1 in third ch from crochet hook, dc14, 3dc in last, continue to crochet along other side of chains, dc15, 3dc in last, sl st in first dc. (36)
Rnd 2: Ch2 (does not count as first st for the entire pattern), dc3, **with light green** dc11, **with dark green** dc3, 2dc in next, dc17, 2dc in next, sl st in first dc. (38)
Rnd 3: With dark green ch2, dc3, **with light green** dc12, **with dark green** dc3, 2dc in next, dc18, 2dc in next, sl st in first dc. (40)
Rnd 4: With dark green ch2, dc3, **with light green** dc13, **with dark green** dc3, 2dc in next, dc19, 2dc in next, sl st in first dc. (42)
Rnd 5: With dark green ch2, dc3, **with light green** dc14, **with dark green** dc3, 2dc in next, dc20, 2dc in next, sl st in first dc. (44)
Rnd 6: With dark green ch2, dc3, **with light green** dc15, **with dark green** dc3, 2dc in next, dc21, 2dc in next, sl st in first dc. (46)
Rnd 7: With dark green ch2, dc3, **with light green** dc16, **with dark green** dc3, 2dc in next, dc22, 2dc in next, sl st in first dc. (48)
Rnd 8: With dark green ch2, dc3, **with light green** dc17, **with dark green** dc3, 2dc in next, dc23, 2dc in next, sl st in first dc. (50)
Rnd 9: With dark green ch2, dc3, **with light green** dc18, **with dark green** dc3, 2dc in next, dc24, 2dc in next, sl st in first dc. (52)
Rnd 10: With dark green ch2, dc3, **with light green** dc19, **with dark green** dc3, 2dc in next, dc25, 2dc in next, sl st in first dc. (54)
Rnd 11: With dark green ch2, dc3, **with light green** dc20, **with dark green** dc3, 2dc in next, dc26, 2dc in next, sl st in first dc. (56)
Rnd 12: With dark green ch2, dc3, **with light green** dc21, **with dark green** dc3, 2dc in next, dc27, 2dc in next, sl st in first dc. (58)
Rnd 13: With dark green ch2, dc3, **with light green** dc22, **with dark green** dc3, 2dc in next, dc28, 2dc in next, sl st in first dc. (60)
Rnd 14: With dark green ch2, dc3, **with light green** dc23, **with dark green** dc3, 2dc in next, dc29, 2dc in next, sl st in first dc. (62)
Rnd 15: With dark green ch2, dc3, **with light green** dc24, **with dark green** dc3, 2dc in next, dc30, 2dc in next, sl st in first dc. (64)
Rnd 16: With dark green ch2, dc3, **with light green** dc25, **with dark green** dc3, 2dc in next, dc31, 2dc in next, sl st in first dc. (66)
Rnd 17: With dark green ch2, dc3, **with light green** dc26, **with dark green** dc3, 2dc in next, dc32, 2dc in next, sl st in first dc. (68)
Rnd 18: With dark green ch2, dc3, **with light green** dc27, **with dark green** dc3, 2dc in next, dc33, 2dc in next, sl st in first dc. (70)
Rnd 19: With dark green ch2, dc3, **with light green** dc28, **with dark green** dc3, 2dc in next, dc34, 2dc in next, sl st in first dc. (72)
Cut a long thread to close the body at the end; fold the body along the increase line.

ARMS (MAKE 2)

Rnd 1: With dark green (leave a long thread here to sew the arm in at the end) ch13, sl st in the first ch to form a ring, ch2 (does not count as first st), dc1 in each ch around, sl st in first dc. (13)
Rnd 2: Ch2, 2dc in first dc, dc1 in each stitch around, sl st in first dc. (14)
Rnd 3: Ch2, dc1 in each stitch all round, sl st in first dc. (14)
Rnd 4: Ch2, 2dc in first dc, dc1 in each stitch round, sl st in first dc. (15)
Rnd 5: Ch2, dc1 in each stitch around, sl st in first dc. (15)
Rnd 6: Ch2, 2dc in first dc, dc1 in each stitch around, sl st in first dc. (16)
Rnd 7: Ch2, dc1 in each stitch around, sl st in first dc. (16)
Rnd 8: Ch2, 2dc in first dc, dc1 in each stitch around, sl st in first dc. (17)
Rnd 9: Ch2, dc1 in each stitch around, sl st in first dc. (17)
Rnd 10: Ch2, 2dc in first dc, dc1 in each stitch around, sl st in first dc. (18)
Rnd 11: From now on, crochet in the round without fastening the rounds, sc1 each stitch around. (18)
Rnd 12: *Sc2, 2sc in next*, repeat from * to * around. (24)
Rnd 13–Rnd 19: Sc1 in each stitch around. (24)
Rnd 20: *Sc1, (in the following stitch: hdc1, dc1, tr1, dc1, hdc1), sc1, sl st*, repeat from * to * around. You will then have three fingers (6 repeats).
Cut a long thread and close the seam of the fingers.

LEGS (MAKE 2)

Rnd 1: With dark green ch14, sl st in the first ch to form a ring, ch2 (does not count as the first stitch), dc1 in each ch around, sl st in first dc. (14)
Rnd 2: Ch2, 2dc in first dc, dc1 in each stitch around, sl st in first dc. (15)
Rnd 3: Ch2, dc1 in each stitch around, sl st in first dc. (15)
Rnd 4: Ch2, 2dc in first dc, dc1 in each stitch around, sl st in first dc. (16)
Rnd 5: Ch2, dc1 in each stitch around, sl st in first dc. (16)
Rnd 6: Ch2, 2dc in first dc, dc1 in each stitch around, sl st in first dc. (17)

Rnd 7: Ch2, dc1 in each stitch around, sl st in first dc. (17)
Rnd 8: Ch2, 2dc in first dc, dc1 in every stitch around, sl st in first dc. (18)
Rnd 9: From now on, crochet in the round without fastening the rounds, sc1 in each stitch around. (18)
Rnd 10: *Sc2, 2sc in next*, repeat from * to * around. (24)
Rnd 11–Rnd 15: Sc1 in each stitch around. (24)
Rnd 16: *Sc1, (in the following stitch: hdc1, dc1, tr1, dc1, hdc1), sc1, sl st*, repeat from * to * around. You will then have three toes (6 repeats).
Cut a long thread and close the toe seam.

PUTTING IT ALL TOGETHER

- Place each leg between the two layers at the bottom of the body. Use the remaining yarn to sew along the bottom with the two feet in between to close the seam while at the same time attaching the parts.
- Sew an arm on either side of the body between Rnd 1 and Rnd 3.
- Sew Rnd 14 of the head on Rnd 1 of the body.

BABY FROG

This baby frog will hop right into your hands for a squeeze.

DIMENSIONS

6.3 in. (16 cm) long and 3.9 in. (10 cm) wide

MATERIALS

DK #3 lightweight yarn (sample shown in Scheepjes Stone Washed):
- light green (New Jade): 55 yd. (50 m)
- dark green (Canada Jade): 109 yd. (100 m)

Crochet hook: US size D-3 (3 mm)
Gold and black safety eyes, 12 mm
Fiberfill stuffing
Needle and scissors

DIFFICULTY LEVEL

EYES (MAKE 2)

Rnd 1: With dark green, start with a magic ring, 6sc in the ring. (6)
Rnd 2: 2sc in each stitch around. (12)
Rnd 3: *Sc2, 2sc in next*, repeat from * to * around. (16)
Rnd 4–Rnd 5: Sc1 in each stitch around. (16)
For the first eye, tie the thread off; for the second eye, let the thread hang and continue with the head.

HEAD

The eyes are connected and form the top of the head.
Rnd 1: With dark green, continue with the second eye, sc7, take the first eye and crochet the next stitch of the second eye and the first eye together, sc14, crochet the next stitch of the first and second eye together, sc7. (30)
Rnd 2: *Sc4, 2sc in next*, repeat from * to * around. (36)
Rnd 3–Rnd 5: Sc1 in each stitch around. (36)
Rnd 6: With dark green sc4, **with light green** sc10, **with dark green** sc22. (36)
Rnd 7: With dark green sc5, **with light green** sc9, **with dark green** sc22. (36)
Rnd 8: With dark green sc6, **with light green** sc8, **with dark green** sc22. (36)
Rnd 9: With dark green sc7, **with light green** sc7, **with dark green** sc22. (36)
Rnd 10: With dark green sc4, sc2tog, sc2, **with light green** sc2, sc2tog, sc2, **with dark green** sc2, sc2tog, *sc4, sc2tog*, repeat from * to * to end. (30)
Rnd 11: With dark green sc3, sc2tog, sc3, **with light green** sc2tog, sc2, **with dark green** sc1, sc2tog, *sc3, sc2tog*, repeat from * to * to end. (24)
Rnd 12: With dark green *sc2, sc2tog*, repeat from * to * 1 more time, **with light green** sc2, **with dark green** sc2tog, *sc2, sc2tog*, repeat from * to * to end. (18)
At this point, attach the eyes between Rnd 5 of the eye and Rnd 1 of the head and fill the head.

Rnd 13: With dark green *sc1, sc2tog*, repeat from * to * 1 more time, sc1, **with light green** sc1, **with dark green** (sc2tog) 2 times, *sc1, sc2tog*, repeat from * to * to end. (12)

Cut the thread, close the seam **with the dark green** thread, and weave in the **light green** thread neatly.

BODY

Rnd 1: With dark green ch13, dc1 in third ch from hook, dc9, 3dc in last ch, continue along other side of chains, dc10, 3dc in last ch, sl st in first dc. (26)

Rnd 2: Ch2 (does not count as first stitch for the entire pattern), *dc12, 2dc in the following*, repeat from * to * 1 more time, sl st in first st. (28)

Rnd 3: Ch2, dc3; **with light green** dc7, **with dark green** dc3, 2dc in next, dc13, 2dc in next, sl st in first dc. (30)

Rnd 4: With dark green ch2, dc3, **with light green** dc8, **with dark green** dc3, 2dc in the next, dc14, 2dc in the next, sl st in first dc. (32)

Rnd 5: With dark green ch2, dc3, **with light green** dc9, **with dark green** dc2, 2dc in next, dc15, 2dc in next, sl st in first dc. (34)

Rnd 6: With dark green ch2, dc3, **with light green** dc10, **with dark green** dc3, 2dc in next, dc16, 2dc in next, sl st in first dc. (36)

Rnd 7: With dark green ch2, dc3, **with light green** dc11, **with dark green** dc3, 2dc in next, dc17, 2dc in next, sl st in first dc. (38)

Rnd 8: With dark green ch2, dc3, **with light green** dc12, **with dark green** dc3, 2dc in next, dc18, 2dc in next, sl st in first dc. (40)

Rnd 9: With dark green ch2, dc3, **with light green** dc13, **with dark green** dc3, 2dc in next, dc19, 2dc in next, sl st in first dc. (42)

Rnd 10: With dark green ch2, dc3, **with light green** dc14, **with dark green** dc3, 2dc in next, dc20, 2dc in next, sl st in first dc. (44)

Rnd 11: With dark green ch2, dc3, **with light green** dc15, **with dark green** dc3, 2dc in next, dc21, 2dc in next, sl st in first dc. (46)

Cut the **light green** thread and weave in the end.

Rnd 12: Ch2, *dc22, ch14, dc1 in third ch from hook, dc1 in each of the 11 remaining chs, 2dc in the next stitch on Rnd 11*, repeat from * to * 1 more time, sl st in first st. Cut a long thread to close the body later.

ARMS (MAKE 2)

Rnd 1: With dark green (leave a long thread here to sew the arm at the end) ch9, sl st in the first ch to form a ring, ch2 (does not count as first dc), dc1 in each ch around, sl st in first dc. (9)

Rnd 2: Ch2, 2dc in first dc, dc1 in each stitch around, sl st in first dc. (10)

Rnd 3: Ch2, dc1 in each stitch around, sl st in first dc. (10)

Rnd 4: Ch2, 2dc in first dc, dc1 in each stitch around, sl st in first dc. (11)

Rnd 5: Ch2, dc1 in each stitch round, sl st in first dc. (11)

Rnd 6: Ch2, 2dc in first dc, dc1 in each stitch around, sl st in first dc. (12)

Rnd 7: From now on hook in continuous rounds without closing the rounds, sc1 in each stitch around. (12)

Rnd 8: *Sc1, 2sc in next*, repeat from * to * around. (18)

Rnd 9–Rnd 10: Sc1 in each stitch around. (18)

Rnd 11: *Sc1, (in next stitch: hdc1, dc1, tr1, dc1, hdc1), sl st *, repeat from * to * all around; you will have three fingers (6 repeats). Cut a long thread and sew the seam of the fingers closed.

PUTTING IT ALL TOGETHER

- Fold the body along the increase lines and use the remaining thread from the body to close the bottom.
- Make a knot in the corners to make the feet.
- Sew an arm on each side of the body between Rnd 1 and Rnd 2.
- Finally, sew Rnd 8 of the head (eyes not counted) to Rnd 1 of the body.

This little one will relax with you anytime.

DIMENSIONS

12.2 in. (31 cm) long and 5.9 in. (15 cm) wide

MATERIALS

DK #3 lightweight yarn (sample shown in Scheepjes Stone Washed):
• purple (Deep Amethyst): 218.7 yd. (200 m)
Crochet hook: US size D-3 (3 mm)
Black and blue safety eyes, 15 mm
Black safety eyes, 10 mm (for nostrils)
Fiberfill stuffing
Yarn needle and scissors

DIFFICULTY LEVEL

HEAD

Rnd 1: Start with a magic ring, 6sc in the loop. (6)
Rnd 2: 2sc in each stitch around. (12)
Rnd 3: *Sc1, 2sc in next*, repeat from * to * around. (18)
Rnd 4: *Sc2, 2sc in next*, repeat from * to * around. (24)
Rnd 5: *Sc3, 2sc in next*, repeat from * to * around. (30)
Rnd 6: *Sc4, 2sc in next*, repeat from * to * around. (36)
Rnd 7: *Sc5, 2sc in next*, repeat from * to * around. (42)
Rnd 8: *Sc6, 2sc in next*, repeat from * to * around. (48)
Rnd 9–Rnd 20: Sc1 in each stitch around. (48)
Rnd 21: *2sc in each of the next 3 stitches, sc21*, repeat from * to * one more time. (54)
Rnd 22: *2sc in each of the next 6 stitches, sc21*, repeat from * to * one more time. (66)
Attach the black and blue safety eyes between Rnd 19 and Rnd 20, 11 stitches apart.
Rnd 23–Rnd 27: Sc1 in each stitch around. (66)
Rnd 28: *Sc9, sc2tog*, repeat from * to * around. (60)
Rnd 29: Sc1 in each stitch around. (60)
Rnd 30: *Sc8, sc2tog*, repeat from * to * around. (54)
Rnd 31: Sc1 in each stitch around. (54)
Rnd 32: *Sc7, sc2tog*, repeat from * to * around. (48)
Rnd 33: *Sc6, sc2tog*, repeat from * to * around. (42)
Rnd 34: *Sc5, sc2tog*, repeat from * to * around. (36)
Rnd 35: *Sc4, sc2tog*, repeat from * to * around. (30)
Rnd 36: *Sc3, sc2tog*, repeat from * to * around. (24)
Rnd 37: *Sc2, sc2tog*, repeat from * to * around. (18)
Attach the nostrils (black safety eyes) between Rnd 30 and Rnd 31, 11 stitches apart; stuff the head.
Rnd 38: *Sc1, sc2tog*, repeat from * to * around. (12)
Cut yarn, close the seam, and weave in ends.

EARS (MAKE 2)

Row 1: Start with a magic ring, 6sc in the loop. (6) You won't close this row, but continue working flat.
Row 2: Turn, ch1 (doesn't count as first stitch for entire ear), sc1, 2dc in each of the next 4 stitches, sc1 in last. (10)
Row 3: Turn, ch1, 2sc in first sc, 1dc in each of the next 8 stitches, 2sc in last. (12)
Cut a long thread, sew ears closed on the bottom (these are the first and last sc of the rows), and attach to each side of the head against Rnd 7.

BODY

Rnd 1: Ch18, 1dc in third ch from hook, dc14, 3dc in last, continue along other side of chains, dc15, 3dc in last, sl st in first dc. (36)
Rnd 2: Ch2 (doesn't count as first stitch now and throughout), *dc17, 2dc in next*, repeat from * to * one more time, sl st in first dc. (38)
Rnd 3: Ch2, *dc18, 2dc in next*, repeat from * to * one more time, sl st in first dc. (40)
Rnd 4: Ch2, *dc19, 2dc in next*, repeat from * to * one more time, sl st in first dc. (42)
Rnd 5: Ch2, *dc20, 2dc in next*, repeat from * to * one more time, sl st in first dc. (44)
Rnd 6: Ch2, *dc21, 2dc in next*, repeat from * to * one more time, sl st in first dc. (46)
Rnd 7: Ch2, *dc22, 2dc in next*, repeat from * to * one more time, sl st in first dc. (48)
Rnd 8: Ch2, *dc23, 2dc in next*, repeat from * to * one more time, sl st in first dc. (50)
Rnd 9: Ch2, *dc24, 2dc in next*, repeat from * to * one more time, sl st in first dc. (52)
Rnd 10: Ch2, *dc25, 2dc in next*, repeat from * to * one more time, sl st in first dc. (54)
Rnd 11: Ch2, *dc26, 2dc in next*, repeat from * to * one more time, sl st in first dc. (56)
Rnd 12: Ch2, *dc27, 2dc in next*, repeat from * to * one more time, sl st in first dc. (58)
Rnd 13: Ch2, *dc28, 2dc in next*, repeat from * to * one more time, sl st in first dc. (60)
Rnd 14: Ch2, *dc29, 2dc in next*, repeat from * to * one more time, sl st in first dc. (62)

Rnd 15: Ch2, *dc30, 2dc in next*, repeat from * to * one more time, sl st in first dc. (64)
Rnd 16: Ch2, *dc31, 2dc in next*, repeat from * to * one more time, sl st in first dc. (66)
Rnd 17: Ch2, *dc32, 2dc in next*, repeat from * to * one more time, sl st in first dc. (68)
Rnd 18: Ch2, *dc33, 2dc in next*, repeat from * to * one more time, sl st in first dc. (70)
Rnd 19: Ch2, *dc34, 2dc in next*, repeat from * to * one more time, sl st in first dc. (72)
Cut a long tail to close the body in the end. Fold the body in line with the increases to make the belly straight.

ARMS (MAKE 2)

Rnd 1: Start with a magic ring, 6sc in the loop. (6)
Rnd 2: 2sc in each stitch around. (12)
Rnd 3: *Sc1, 2sc in next*, repeat from * to * around. (18)
Rnd 4: *Sc2, 2sc in next*, repeat from * to * around. (24)
Rnd 5–Rnd 9: Sc1 in each stitch around. (24)
Rnd 10: *Sc2, sc2tog*, repeat from * to * around. (18)
Rnd 11–Rnd 12: Sc1 in each stitch around. (18)
Rnd 13: Sl st, ch2 (doesn't count as first stitch now and throughout), dc1 in each stitch around, sl st in first dc. (18)
Rnd 14: Ch2, dc2tog, dc1 in each stitch around, sl st in first dc. (17)
At this point, stuff the hand, take a piece of purple yarn, and sew across the arm between Rnd 12 and Rnd 13.
Rnd 15: Ch2, dc1 in each stitch around, sl st in first dc. (17)
Rnd 16: Ch2, dc2tog, dc1 in each stitch around, sl st in first dc. (16)
Rnd 17: Ch2, dc1 in each stitch around, sl st in first dc. (16)
Rnd 18: Ch2, dc2tog, dc1 in each stitch around, sl st in first dc. (15)
Rnd 19: Ch2, dc1 in each stitch around, sl st in first dc. (15)
Rnd 20: Ch2, dc2tog, dc1 in each stitch around, sl st in first dc. (14)
Rnd 21: Ch2, dc1 in each stitch around, sl st in first dc. (14)
Rnd 22: Ch2, dc2tog, dc1 in each stitch around, sl st in first dc. (13) Cut a long tail to attach arms later.

FEET (MAKE 2)

Rnd 1: Start with a magic ring, ch2 (doesn't count as first stitch now and throughout), 12dc in the loop, sl st in first dc. (12)
Rnd 2: Ch2, *dc1, 2dc in next*, repeat around from * to *, sl st in first dc. (18)
Rnd 3–Rnd 7: Ch2, dc1 in each stitch around, sl st in first dc. (18) Cut the yarn and weave in ends.

PUTTING IT ALL TOGETHER

- Place both legs between the bottom two layers of the body and use the remaining yarn from the body to sew across the seam, with legs in between, to close and at the same time attach the parts.
- Sew an arm to each side of the body between Rnd 1 and Rnd 3.
- Sew Rnd 25 of the head to Rnd 1 of the body.

HIPPO CALF

This little hippo is ready to play by the water instead of in it.

DIMENSIONS

6.7 in. (17 cm) long and 3.9 in. (10 cm) wide

MATERIALS

DK #3 lightweight yarn (sample shown in Scheepjes Stone Washed):
• purple (Lilac Quartz): 142.2 yd. (130 m)
Crochet hook: US size D-3 (3 mm)
Blue and black safety eyes, 15 mm
Fiberfill stuffing
Yarn needle and scissors

DIFFICULTY LEVEL

HEAD

Rnd 1: Start with a magic ring, 6sc in the ring. (6)
Rnd 2: 2sc in each stitch around. (12)
Rnd 3: *Sc1, 2sc in next*, repeat from * to * around. (18)
Rnd 4: *Sc2, 2sc in next*, repeat from * to * around. (24)
Rnd 5: *Sc3, 2sc in next*, repeat from * to * around. (30)
Rnd 6: *Sc4, 2sc in next*, repeat from * to * around. (36)
Rnd 7–Rnd 14: Sc1 in each stitch around. (36)
Rnd 15: *2sc in each of the following 2 stitches, sc16*, repeat from * to * 1 more time. (40)
Rnd 16: *2sc in each of the following 4 stitches, sc16*, repeat from * to * 1 more time. (48)
Attach the blue and black eyes between Rnd 14 and Rnd 15 with 7 stitches in between.
Rnd 17–Rnd 18: Sc1 in each stitch around. (48)
Rnd 19: *Sc6, sc2tog*, repeat from * to * around. (42)
Rnd 20: Sc1 in each stitch around. (42)
Rnd 21: *Sc5, sc2tog*, repeat from * to * around. (36)
Rnd 22: Sc1 in each stitch around. (36)
Rnd 23: *Sc4, sc2tog*, repeat from * to * around. (30)
Rnd 24: *Sc3, sc2tog*, repeat from * to * around. (24)
Rnd 25: *Sc2, sc2tog*, repeat from * to * around. (18)
Now attach the black safety eyes for the nostrils between Rnd 21 and Rnd 22 with 7 stitches in between and fill the head.
Rnd 26: *Sc1, sc2tog*, repeat from * to * around. (12)
Cut the thread, close the seam, and weave in the yarn.

EARS (MAKE 2)

Start with a magic ring, 6sc in the ring; do not close this rnd, but turn and work back. (6)
Ch1 (does not count as first stitch), sc1, 2dc in each of the 4 following stitches, sc1 in the last. (10)
Cut a long thread and sew up the ears at the bottom (the first and the last sc of the rows). Let the yarn hang to secure the ears later.

BODY

Rnd 1: Ch13, dc1 in third ch from hook, dc9, 3dc in last, continue along other side of chains, dc10, 3dc in last, sl st in first dc. (26)
Rnd 2: Ch2 (does not count as the first dc from now on), *dc12, 2dc in the next*, repeat from * to * 1 more time, sl st in first dc. (28)
Rnd 3: Ch2, *dc13, 2dc in next*, repeat from * to * 1 more time, sl st in first dc. (30)
Rnd 4: Ch2, *dc14, 2dc in next*, repeat from * to * 1 more time, sl st in first dc. (32)
Rnd 5: Ch2, *dc15, 2dc in next*, repeat from * to * 1 more time, sl st in first dc. (34)
Rnd 6: Ch2, *dc16, 2dc in next*, repeat from * to * 1 more time, sl st in first dc. (36)
Rnd 7: Ch2, *dc17, 2dc in next*, repeat from * to * 1 more time, sl st in first dc. (38)
Rnd 8: Ch2, *dc18, 2dc in next*, repeat from * to * 1 more time, sl st in first dc. (40)
Rnd 9: Ch2, *dc19, 2dc in next*, repeat from * to * 1 more time, sl st in first dc. (42)
Rnd 10: Ch2, *dc20, 2dc in next*, repeat from * to * 1 more time, sl st in first dc. (44)
Rnd 11: Ch2, *dc21, 2dc in next*, repeat from * to * 1 more time, sl st in first dc. (46)
Rnd 12: Ch2, *dc22, ch14, dc1 in 3rd ch from hook, dc1 in each of the 11 remaining chs, 2dc in the next stitch on Rnd 11*, repeat from * to * 1 more time, sl st in first st.
Cut a long thread to close the body later.

ARMS (MAKE 2)

Rnd 1: Start with a magic ring, 6sc in the ring. (6)
Rnd 2: 2sc in each stitch around. (12)
Rnd 3: *Sc1, 2sc in next*, repeat from * to * around. (18)
Rnd 4–Rnd 5: Sc1 in each stitch around. (18)
Rnd 6: *Sc1, sc2tog*, repeat from * to * around. (12)
Rnd 7: Sc1 in each stitch around. (12)
Rnd 8: Sl st, ch2 (does not count as first dc from now on), dc1 in every stitch around, sl st in first dc. (12)
Rnd 9: Ch2, dc2tog, dc1 in each stitch around, sl st in first dc. (11)
Now stuff the hand, and then take a piece of yarn and sew along the hand between Rnd 7 and Rnd 8.
Rnd 10: Ch2, dc1 in each stitch around, sl st in first dc. (11)
Rnd 11: Ch2, dc2tog, dc1 in each stitch around, sl st in first dc. (10)
Rnd 12: Ch2, dc1 in each stitch around, sl st in first dc. (10)
Rnd 13: Ch2, dc2tog, dc1 in each stitch around, sl st in first dc. (9)
Cut and leave a long thread to secure the arms later.

PUTTING IT ALL TOGETHER

- Sew the ears to the sides of the head in Rnd 5.
- Fold the body neatly on the increase lines and close the bottom.
- Make a knot in the corners to make the feet.
- Sew an arm on each side of the body between Rnd 1 and Rnd 2.
- Sew Rnd 23 of the head to Rnd 1 of the body.

KANGAROO

This mama kangaroo has a pouch for her joey or a secret treasure.

DIMENSIONS

11.4 in. (29 cm) long and 6.3 in. (16 cm) wide

MATERIALS

DK #3 lightweight yarn (sample shown in Scheepjes Stone Washed):
- beige (Boulder Opal): 218.7 yd. (200 m)
- white (Moon Stone): 76.6 yd. (70 m)

Crochet hook: US size D-3 (3 mm)
Black safety eyes, 15 mm
Black safety nose, 15 mm
Fiberfill stuffing
Yarn needle and scissors

DIFFICULTY LEVEL

HEAD

Rnd 1: With beige, start with a magic ring, 6sc in the loop. (6)
Rnd 2: 2sc in each stitch around. (12)
Rnd 3: *Sc1, 2sc in next*, repeat from * to * around. (18)
Rnd 4: *Sc2, 2sc in next*, repeat from * to * around. (24)
Rnd 5: *Sc3, 2sc in next*, repeat from * to * around. (30)
Rnd 6: *Sc4, 2sc in next*, repeat from * to * around. (36)
Rnd 7: *Sc5, 2sc in next*, repeat from * to * around. (42)
Rnd 8–Rnd 15: Sc1 in each stitch around. (42)
Rnd 16: 3sc in next stitch, sc3, 3sc in next stitch, sc37. (46)
Rnd 17: Sc1, 3sc in next stitch, sc5, 3sc in next stitch, sc38. (50)
Rnd 18: Sc2, 3sc in next stitch, sc7, 3sc in next stitch, sc39. (54)
Rnd 19–Rnd 23: Sc1 in each stitch around. (54)
Attach the safety eyes between Rnd 15 and Rnd 16 on both sides of the snout with 8 stitches between them.
Attach the safety nose between Rnd 20 and Rnd 21 in the center of the snout.
Rnd 24: *Sc7, sc2tog*, repeat from * to * around. (48)
Rnd 25: *Sc6, sc2tog*, repeat from * to * around. (42)
Rnd 26: *Sc5, sc2tog*, repeat from * to * around. (36)
Rnd 27: *Sc4, sc2tog*, repeat from * to * around. (30)
Rnd 28: *Sc3, sc2tog*, repeat from * to * around. (24)
Rnd 29: *Sc2, sc2tog*, repeat from * to * around. (18)
Stuff the head.
Rnd 30: *Sc1, sc2tog*, repeat from * to * around. (12)
Cut a long thread, close the seam, and weave in ends.

EARS (MAKE 2)

Rnd 1: With beige, start with a magic ring, ch2 (doesn't count as first dc now and throughout), 12dc in the loop, sl st in first dc. (12)
Rnd 2: Ch2, dc1, 5dc in next, dc4, 5dc in next, dc4, 5dc in next, sl st in first dc. (24)
Rnd 3: Ch2, dc3, 5dc in next, dc8, 5dc in next, dc8, 5dc in next, dc2, sl st in first dc. (36)
Cut a long thread, fold the bottom (the side with the least dc, so the side where your yarn is attached), and sew the bottom closed; let the yarn end hang to attach ears later.

BODY

Rnd 1: With beige ch18, 1dc in third ch from hook, dc14, 3dc in last, continue along other side of chains, dc15, 3dc in last, sl st in first dc. (36)
Rnd 2: Ch2 (doesn't count as first dc now and throughout), dc3, **with white** dc11, **with beige** dc3, 2dc in next, dc17, 2dc in next, sl st in first dc. (38)
Rnd 3: With beige ch2, dc3, **with white** dc12, **with beige** dc3, 2dc in next, dc18, 2dc in next, sl st in first dc. (40)
Rnd 4: With beige ch2, dc3, **with white** dc13, **with beige** dc3, 2dc in next, dc19, 2dc in next, sl st in first dc. (42)
Rnd 5: With beige ch2, dc3, **with white** dc14, **with beige** dc3, 2dc in next, dc20, 2dc in next, sl st in first dc. (44)
Rnd 6: With beige ch2, dc3, **with white** dc15, **with beige** dc3, 2dc in next, dc21, 2dc in next, sl st in first dc. (46)
Rnd 7: With beige ch2, dc3, **with white** dc16, **with beige** dc3, 2dc in next, dc22, 2dc in next, sl st in first dc. (48)
Rnd 8: With beige ch2, dc3, **with white** dc17, **with beige** dc3, 2dc in next, dc23, 2dc in next, sl st in first dc. (50)
Rnd 9: With beige ch2, dc3, **with white** dc18, **with beige** dc3, 2dc in next, dc24, 2dc in next, sl st in first dc. (52)
Rnd 10: With beige ch2, dc3, **with white** dc19, **with beige** dc3, 2dc in next, dc25, 2dc in next, sl st in first dc. (54)
Rnd 11: With beige ch2, dc3, **with white** dc20, **with beige** dc3, 2dc in next, dc26, 2dc in next, sl st in first dc. (56)
Rnd 12: With beige ch2, dc3, **with white** dc21, **with beige** dc3, 2dc in next, dc27, 2dc in next, sl st in first dc. (58)
Rnd 13: With beige ch2, dc3, **with white** dc22, **with beige** dc3, 2dc in next, dc28, 2dc in next, sl st in first dc. (60)
From now on you'll continue with beige; you can cut the white yarn.
Rnd 14: Ch2, *dc29, 2dc in next*, repeat from * to * one more time, sl st in first dc. (62)
Rnd 15: Ch2, *dc30, 2dc in next*, repeat from * to * one more time, sl st in first dc. (64)
Rnd 16: Ch2, *dc31, 2dc in next*, repeat from * to * one more time, sl st in first dc. (66)
Rnd 17: Ch2, *dc32, 2dc in next*, repeat from * to * one more time, sl st in first dc. (68)
Rnd 18: Ch2, *dc33, 2dc in next*, repeat from * to * one more time, sl st in first dc. (70)
Rnd 19: Ch2, *dc34, 2dc in next*, repeat from * to * one more time, sl st in first dc. (72)
Rnd 20: Ch2, *dc35, 2dc in next*, repeat from * to * one more time, sl st in first dc. (74)
Rnd 21: Ch2, *dc36, 2dc in next*, repeat from * to * one more time, sl st in first dc. (76)
Cut a long thread to close the body in the end; fold the body in line with the increases on the side.

ARMS (MAKE 2)

Rnd 1: With beige, start with a magic ring, 6sc in the loop. (6)
Rnd 2: 2sc in each stitch around. (12)
Rnd 3: *Sc1, 2sc in next*, repeat from * to * around. (18)
Rnd 4: *Sc2, 2sc in next*, repeat from * to * around. (24)
Rnd 5–Rnd 9: Sc1 in each stitch around. (24)
Rnd 10: *Sc2, sc2tog*, repeat from * to * around. (18)
Rnd 11–Rnd 12: Sc1 in each stitch around. (18)
Cut a long thread; you'll use it after Rnd 14.
Rnd 13: Sl st 1, ch2 (doesn't count as first stitch now and throughout), dc1 in each stitch around, sl st in first dc. (18)
Rnd 14: Ch2, dc2tog, dc1 in each stitch around, sl st in first dc. (17)
At this point, stuff the hand. Take the remaining yarn and sew across the arm between Rnd 12 and Rnd 13.
Rnd 15: Ch2, dc1 in each stitch around, sl st in first dc. (17)
Rnd 16: Ch2, dc2tog, dc1 in each stitch around, sl st in first dc. (16)
Rnd 17: Ch2, dc1 in each stitch around, sl st in first dc. (16)
Rnd 18: Ch2, dc2tog, dc1 in each stitch around, sl st in first dc. (15)
Rnd 19: Ch2, dc1 in each stitch around, sl st in first dc. (15)
Rnd 20: Ch2, dc2tog, dc1 in each stitch around, sl st in first dc. (14)
Rnd 21: Ch2, dc1 in each stitch around, sl st in first dc. (14)
Rnd 22: Ch2, dc2tog, dc1 in each stitch around, sl st in first dc. (13)
Cut a long tail to attach the arms to the body later.

LEGS (MAKE 2)

Rnd 1: With beige, start with a magic ring, ch2 (doesn't count as first stitch now and throughout), dc12 in the loop, sl st in first dc. (12)
Rnd 2: Ch2, *dc1, 2dc in next*, repeat from * to * around, sl st in first dc. (18)
Rnd 3–Rnd 4: Ch2, dc1 in each stitch around, sl st in first dc. (18)
Cut the yarn and weave in the ends.

POUCH

Note: This isn't crocheted in the round.

Row 1: With beige, start with a magic ring, ch2 (doesn't count as first stitch now and throughout), dc8. (8)

Row 2: Ch2, turn, dc1, 2dc in each of the next 6dc, dc1. (14)

Row 3: Ch2, turn, dc1, *dc1, 2dc in next*, repeat from * to * 5 more times, dc1. (20)

Row 4: Ch2, turn, dc1, *dc2, 2dc in next*, repeat from * to * 5 more times, dc1. (26)

Row 5: Ch2, turn, dc1, *dc3, 2dc in next*, repeat from * to * 5 more times, dc1. (32)

Row 6: Ch2, turn, dc1, *dc4, 2dc in next*, repeat from * to * 5 more times, dc1. (38)

Row 7: Instead of turning, continue along the top side of the pouch; this is actually on the side of the rows you just made, ch3, 2dc on the side of each row (you'll crochet this around the side of the double crochets and the chain twos on the side). End with 1dc in the first dc of row 6.

Cut a long thread to attach the pouch to the body in the end.

TAIL

Rnd 1: With beige, start with a magic ring, ch2 (doesn't count as first stitch now and throughout), 12dc in the loop, sl st in first dc. (12)

Rnd 2: Ch2, *dc3, 5dc in next*, repeat from * to * around, sl st in first dc. (24)

Rnd 3: Ch2, dc5, 5dc in next, *dc7, 5dc in next*, repeat from * to * 1 more time, dc2, sl st in first dc. (36)

Rnd 4: Ch2, dc7, 5dc in next, *dc11, 5dc in next*, repeat from * to * 1 more time, dc4, sl st in first dc. (48)

Rnd 5: Ch2, dc9, 5dc in next, *dc15, 5dc in next*, repeat from * to * 1 more time, dc6, sl st in first dc. (60)

Rnd 6: Ch2, dc11, 5dc in next, *dc19, 5dc in next*, repeat from * to * 1 more time, dc8, sl st in first dc. (72)

Cut a long thread to close the tail and attach it to the body in the end.

PUTTING IT ALL TOGETHER

- Sew the pouch to the belly from Rnd 13 to Rnd 21.
- Place both legs in the bottom two layers of the body. With the remaining yarn from the body, sew across the seam with the parts in between. This way you close the bottom and assemble the pieces at the same time.
- Sew an arm to each side of the body between Rnd 1 and Rnd 3.
- Sew the ears to each side of the head in Rnd 7; they are 6 stitches apart on the back.
- Fold the tail in half, sew closed, and sew the tail to the bottom 6 rounds of the body.
- Finally, sew Rnd 24 of the head to Rnd 1 of the body.

2500g
500g
1500g

2900
100
200
2800
300
2700
3
Kg
2600
400
3kg
10g
2500g
500g
2400
600
2300
700
2200
800
2100
900
2
Kg
1
Kg
1900
1100
1800
1200
1700
1500g
1300
1600
1400

JOEY

DIMENSIONS

6.3 in. (16 cm) long by 3.9 in. (10 cm) wide

MATERIALS

DK #3 lightweight yarn (sample shown in Scheepjes Stone Washed):
- beige (Boulder Opal): 142.2 yd. (130 m)

Crochet hook: US size D-3 (3 mm)
Black safety eyes, 12 mm
Black safety nose, 15 mm
Fiberfill stuffing
Yarn needle and scissors

DIFFICULTY LEVEL

HEAD

Rnd 1: Start with a magic ring, 6sc in the loop. (6)
Rnd 2: 2sc in each stitch around. (12)
Rnd 3: *Sc1, 2sc in next*, repeat from * to * around. (18)
Rnd 4: *Sc2, 2sc in next*, repeat from * to * around. (24)
Rnd 5: *Sc3, 2sc in next*, repeat from * to * around. (30)
Rnd 6–Rnd 10: Sc1 in each stitch around. (30)
Rnd 11: 3sc in next stitch, sc1, 3sc in next stitch, sc27. (34)
Rnd 12: Sc1, 3sc in next stitch, sc3, 3sc in next stitch, sc28. (38)
Rnd 13: Sc2, 3sc in next stitch, sc5, 3sc in next stitch, sc29. (42)
Rnd 14–Rnd 17: Sc1 in each stitch around. (42)
Attach the safety eyes between Rnd 10 and Rnd 11 on each side of the snout with 6 stitches between them.
Attach the safety nose between Rnd 14 and Rnd 15 in the center of the snout.
Rnd 18: *Sc5, sc2tog*, repeat from * to * around. (36)
Rnd 19: *Sc4, sc2tog*, repeat from * to * around. (30)
Rnd 20: *Sc3, sc2tog*, repeat from * to * around. (24)
Rnd 21: *Sc2, sc2tog*, repeat from * to * around. (18)
Cut a long thread, close the seam, and weave in the ends.

EARS (MAKE 2)

Rnd 1: Start with a magic ring, ch2 (doesn't count as first dc now and throughout), 12dc in the loop, sl st in first dc. (12)
Rnd 2: Ch2, dc1, 5dc in next, dc4, 5dc in next, dc4, 5dc in next, sl st in first dc. (24)
Cut a long thread, fold the bottom (the side where your yarn is attached), and sew the bottom closed; let the yarn end hang to attach the ears later.

BODY

Rnd 1: Ch13, dc1 in third ch from hook, dc9, 3dc in last, continue along other side of chains, dc10, 3dc in last, sl st in first dc. (26)
Rnd 2: Ch2 (doesn't count as first stitch now and throughout), *dc12, 2dc in next* repeat from * to * one more time, sl st in first dc. (28)
Rnd 3: Ch2, *dc13, 2dc in next*, repeat from * to * one more time, sl st in first dc. (30)
Rnd 4: Ch2, *dc14, 2dc in next*, repeat from * to * one more time, sl st in first dc. (32)
Rnd 5: Ch2, *dc15, 2dc in next*, repeat from * to * one more time, sl st in first dc. (34)
Rnd 6: Ch2, *dc16, 2dc in next*, repeat from * to * one more time, sl st in first dc. (36)
Rnd 7: Ch2, *dc17, 2dc in next*, repeat from * to * one more time, sl st in first dc. (38)
Rnd 8: Ch2, *dc18, 2dc in next*, repeat from * to * one more time, sl st in first dc. (40)
Rnd 9: Ch2, *dc19, 2dc in next*, repeat from * to * one more time, sl st in first dc. (42)
Rnd 10: Ch2, *dc20, 2dc in next*, repeat from * to * one more time, sl st in first dc. (44)
Rnd 11: Ch2, *dc21, 2dc in next*, repeat from * to * one more time, sl st in first dc. (46)
Rnd 12: Ch2, *dc22, ch14, dc1 in third ch from hook, dc1 in each of the remaining 11 chains, 2dc in next stitch of Rnd 11*, repeat from * to * one more time, sl st in first dc. Cut a long tail to close the body later.

ARMS (MAKE 2)

Rnd 1: Start with a magic ring, 6sc in the loop. (6)
Rnd 2: 2sc in each stitch around. (12)
Rnd 3: *Sc1, 2sc in next*, repeat from * to * around. (18)
Rnd 4–Rnd 5: Sc1 in each stitch around. (18)
Rnd 6: *Sc1, sc2tog*, repeat from * to * around. (12)
Rnd 7: Sc1 in each stitch around. (12) Cut a long thread; you'll use it after Rnd 9.
Rnd 8: Sl st 1, ch2 (doesn't count as first stitch now and throughout), dc1 in each stitch around, sl st in first dc. (12)
Rnd 9: Ch2, dc2tog, dc1 in each stitch around, sl st in first dc. (11)
At this point, stuff the hand. Take the remaining yarn and sew across the arm between Rnd 7 and Rnd 8.
Rnd 10: Ch2, dc1 in each stitch around, sl st in first dc. (11)
Rnd 11: Ch2, dc2tog, dc1 in each stitch around, sl st in first dc. (10)
Rnd 12: Ch2, dc1 in each stitch around, sl st in first dc. (10)
Rnd 13: Ch2, dc2tog, dc1 in each stitch around, sl st in first dc. (9)
Cut a long tail to attach the arms to the body later.

TAIL

Rnd 1: Start with a magic ring, ch2 (doesn't count as first stitch now and throughout), dc12 in the loop, sl st in first dc. (12)
Rnd 2: Ch2, *dc3, 5dc in next*, repeat from * to * around, sl st in first dc. (24)
Rnd 3: Ch2, dc5, 5dc in next, *dc7, 5dc in next*, repeat from * to * 1 more time, dc2, sl st in first dc. (36)
Cut a long thread to close the tail and to attach it to the body in the end.

PUTTING IT ALL TOGETHER

- Fold the body in line with the increases to make the belly straight; sew closed with the remaining yarn. Tie a knot in the corners to form the feet.
- Sew an arm to each side of the body between Rnd 1 and Rnd 3.
- Sew an ear to each side of the head in Rnd 4; on the back they are 6 stitches apart.
- Fold the tail in half, sew closed, and then sew the tail to the body from Rnd 9 to Rnd 11.
- Finally, sew Rnd 18 of the head to Rnd 1 of the body.

You will want to share a banana with this cute monkey.

DIMENSIONS

11 in. (28 cm) long and 5.9 in. (15 cm) wide

MATERIALS

DK #3 lightweight yarn (sample shown in Scheepjes Stone Washed):
- brown (Brown Agate): 218.7 yd. (200 m)
- pink (Pink Quartzite): 76.6 yd. (70 m)

Crochet hook: US size D-3 (3 mm)
Black and blue safety eyes, 15 mm
Fiberfill stuffing
Yarn needle and scissors

DIFFICULTY LEVEL

HEAD

Rnd 1: With brown, start with a magic ring, 6sc in the loop. (6)
Rnd 2: 2sc in each stitch around. (12)
Rnd 3: *Sc1, 2sc in next*, repeat from * to * around. (18)
Rnd 4: *Sc2, 2sc in next*, repeat from * to * around. (24)
Rnd 5: *Sc3, 2sc in next*, repeat from * to * around. (30)
Rnd 6: *Sc4, 2sc in next*, repeat from * to * around. (36)
Rnd 7: *Sc5, 2sc in next*, repeat from * to * around. (42)
Rnd 8: *Sc6, 2sc in next*, repeat from * to * around. (48)
Rnd 9: *Sc7, 2sc in next*, repeat from * to * around. (54)
Rnd 10–Rnd 12: Sc1 in each stitch around. (54)
Rnd 13: With brown sc6, **with pink** sc3, **with brown** sc9, **with pink** sc3, **with brown** sc33. (54)
Rnd 14: With brown sc5, **with pink** sc5, **with brown** sc7, **with pink** sc5, **with brown** sc32. (54)
Rnd 15: With brown sc4, **with pink** sc7, **with brown** sc5, **with pink** sc7, **with brown** sc31. (54)
Rnd 16: With brown sc3, **with pink** sc9, **with brown** sc3, **with pink** sc9, **with brown** sc30. (54)
Rnd 17: With brown sc3, **with pink** sc10, **with brown** sc1, **with pink** sc11, **with brown** sc29. (54)
Rnd 18: With brown sc3, **with pink** sc23, **with brown** sc28. (54)
Rnd 19: With brown sc2tog, sc1, **with pink** sc6, sc2tog, sc7, sc2tog, sc6, **with brown** sc1, *sc2tog, sc7*, repeat from * to * to end. (48)
Rnd 20: With brown sc2tog, sc1, **with pink** sc5, sc2tog, sc6, sc2tog, sc5, **with brown** sc1, *sc2tog, sc6*, repeat from * to * to end. (42)
Rnd 21: With brown sc2tog, sc1, **with pink** sc4, sc2tog, sc5, sc2tog, sc4, **with brown** sc1, *sc2tog, sc5*, repeat from * to * to end. (36)
Rnd 22: With brown sc2tog, sc1, **with pink** sc3, sc2tog, sc4, sc2tog, sc3, **with brown** sc1, *sc2tog, sc4*, repeat from * to * to end. (30)
Rnd 23: With brown sc2tog, sc1, **with pink** sc2, sc2tog, sc3, sc2tog, sc2, **with brown** sc1, *sc2tog, sc3*, repeat from * to * to end. (24)

Rnd 24: With brown sc2tog, sc1, **with pink** sc1, sc2tog, sc2, sc2tog, sc1, **with brown** sc1, *sc2tog, sc2*, repeat from * to * to end. (18)

Attach safety eyes between Rnd 18 and Rnd 19 and stuff the head.

Rnd 25: With brown sc2tog, sc1, **with pink** sc2tog, sc1, sc2tog, **with brown** sc1, *sc2tog, sc1*, repeat from * to * to end. (12)

Cut yarn, close the seam with the brown thread, and weave in the pink thread.

SNOUT

Rnd 1: With pink, start with a magic ring, 6sc in the loop. (6)

Rnd 2: 2sc in each stitch around. (12)

Rnd 3: *Sc1, 2sc in next*, repeat from * to * around. (18)

Rnd 4: *Sc2, 2sc in next*, repeat from * to * around. (24)

Rnd 5: *Sc3, 2sc in next*, repeat from * to * around. (30)

Rnd 6–Rnd 8: Sc1 in each stitch around. (30)

Cut a long thread to attach the snout to the face. Make sure it's centered between the eyes and sew between Rnd 19 and Rnd 25 of the head; when the seam is almost completely sewn, you can stuff the snout and sew it closed.

EARS (MAKE 2)

Rnd 1: With brown, start with a magic ring, 6sc in the loop. (6)

Rnd 2: Sc2, 2dc in each of the next 4 stitches. (10)

Rnd 3: Sc2, 2dc in each of the next 8 stitches. (18)

Cut a long thread and sew the 2sc of Rnd 3 of the ears to Rnd 15–Rnd 17 of the head.

BODY

Rnd 1: With brown ch18, 1dc in third ch from hook, dc14, 3dc in last, continue along other side of chains, dc15, 3dc in last, sl st in first dc. (36)

Rnd 2: Ch2 (doesn't count as first stitch now and throughout), *dc17, 2dc in next*, repeat from * to * one more time, sl st in first dc. (38)

Rnd 3: Ch2, *dc18, 2dc in next*, repeat from * to * one more time, sl st in first dc. (40)

Rnd 4: Ch2, *dc19, 2dc in next*, repeat from * to * one more time, sl st in first dc. (42)

Rnd 5: Ch2, *dc20, 2dc in next*, repeat from * to * one more time, sl st in first dc. (44)

Rnd 6: Ch2, *dc21, 2dc in next*, repeat from * to * one more time, sl st in first dc. (46)

Rnd 7: Ch2, *dc22, 2dc in next*, repeat from * to * one more time, sl st in first dc. (48)

Rnd 8: Ch2, *dc23, 2dc in next*, repeat from * to * one more time, sl st in first dc. (50)

Rnd 9: Ch2, *dc24, 2dc in next*, repeat from * to * one more time, sl st in first dc. (52)

Rnd 10: Ch2, *dc25, 2dc in next*, repeat from * to * one more time, sl st in first dc. (54)

Rnd 11: Ch2, *dc26, 2dc in next*, repeat from * to * one more time, sl st in first dc. (56)

Rnd 12: Ch2, *dc27, 2dc in next*, repeat from * to * one more time, sl st in first dc. (58)

Rnd 13: Ch2, *dc28, 2dc in next*, repeat from * to * one more time, sl st in first dc. (60)

Rnd 14: Ch2, *dc29, 2dc in next*, repeat from * to * one more time, sl st in first dc. (62)

Rnd 15: Ch2, *dc30, 2dc in next*, repeat from * to * one more time, sl st in first dc. (64)

Rnd 16: Ch2, *dc31, 2dc in next*, repeat from * to * one more time, sl st in first dc. (66)

Rnd 17: Ch2, *dc32, 2dc in next*, repeat from * to * one more time, sl st in first dc. (68)

Rnd 18: Ch2, *dc33, 2dc in next*, repeat from * to * one more time, sl st in first dc. (70)

Rnd 19: Ch2, *dc34, 2dc in next*, repeat from * to * one more time, sl st in first dc. (72)

Cut a long tail to close the body in the end. Fold the body in line with the increases to make the belly straight.

ARMS (MAKE 2)

Rnd 1: With brown, start with a magic ring, 6sc in the loop. (6)

Rnd 2: 2sc in each stitch around. (12)

Rnd 3: *Sc1, 2sc in next*, repeat from * to * around. (18)

Rnd 4: *Sc2, 2sc in next*, repeat from * to * around. (24)

Rnd 5–Rnd 9: Sc1 in each stitch around. (24)

Rnd 10: *Sc2, sc2tog*, repeat from * to * around. (18)

Rnd 11–Rnd 12: Sc1 in each stitch around. (18)

Rnd 13: Sl st, ch2 (doesn't count as first stitch now and throughout), dc1 in each stitch around, sl st in first dc. (18)

Rnd 14: Ch2, dc2tog, dc1 in each stitch around, sl st in first dc. (17)

At this point, stuff the hand and, with a piece of brown yarn, sew across the arm between Rnd 12 and Rnd 13.

Rnd 15: Ch2, dc1 in each stitch around, sl st in first dc. (17)

Rnd 16: Ch2, dc2tog, dc1 in each stitch around, sl st in first dc. (16)

Rnd 17: Ch2, dc1 in each stitch around, sl st in first dc. (16)

Rnd 18: Ch2, dc2tog, dc1 in each stitch around, sl st in first dc. (15)

Rnd 19: Ch2, dc1 in each stitch around, sl st in first dc. (15)

Rnd 20: Ch2, dc2tog, dc1 in each stitch around, sl st in first dc. (14)

Rnd 21: Ch2, dc1 in each stitch around, sl st in first dc. (14)

Rnd 22: Ch2, dc2tog, dc1 in each stitch around, sl st in first dc. (13)

Cut a long tail to attach the arms later.

LEGS (MAKE 2)

Rnd 1: With brown, start with a magic ring, ch2 (doesn't count as first stitch now and throughout), 12dc in the loop, sl st in first dc. (12)
Rnd 2: Ch2, *dc1, 2dc in next*, repeat from * to * around, sl st in first dc. (18)
Rnd 3–Rnd 7: Ch2, dc1 in each stitch around, sl st in first dc. (18)
Cut the yarn and weave in the ends.

TAIL

Rnd 1: With brown, start with a magic ring, ch2 (doesn't count as first stitch now and throughout), 6dc in the loop, sl st in first dc. (6)
Rnd 2–Rnd 10: Ch2, dc1 in each stitch around, sl st in first dc. (6)
Cut the yarn and weave in the ends.

PUTTING IT ALL TOGETHER

- Place both legs and the tail between the bottom two layers of the body; use the remaining yarn from the body to sew across the seam, with the legs and tail in between, to close and at the same time attach the parts.
- Sew an arm to each side of the body between Rnd 1 and Rnd 3.
- Sew Rnd 21 of the head to Rnd 1 of the body.

BABY MONKEY

Would you like to share a banana with me?

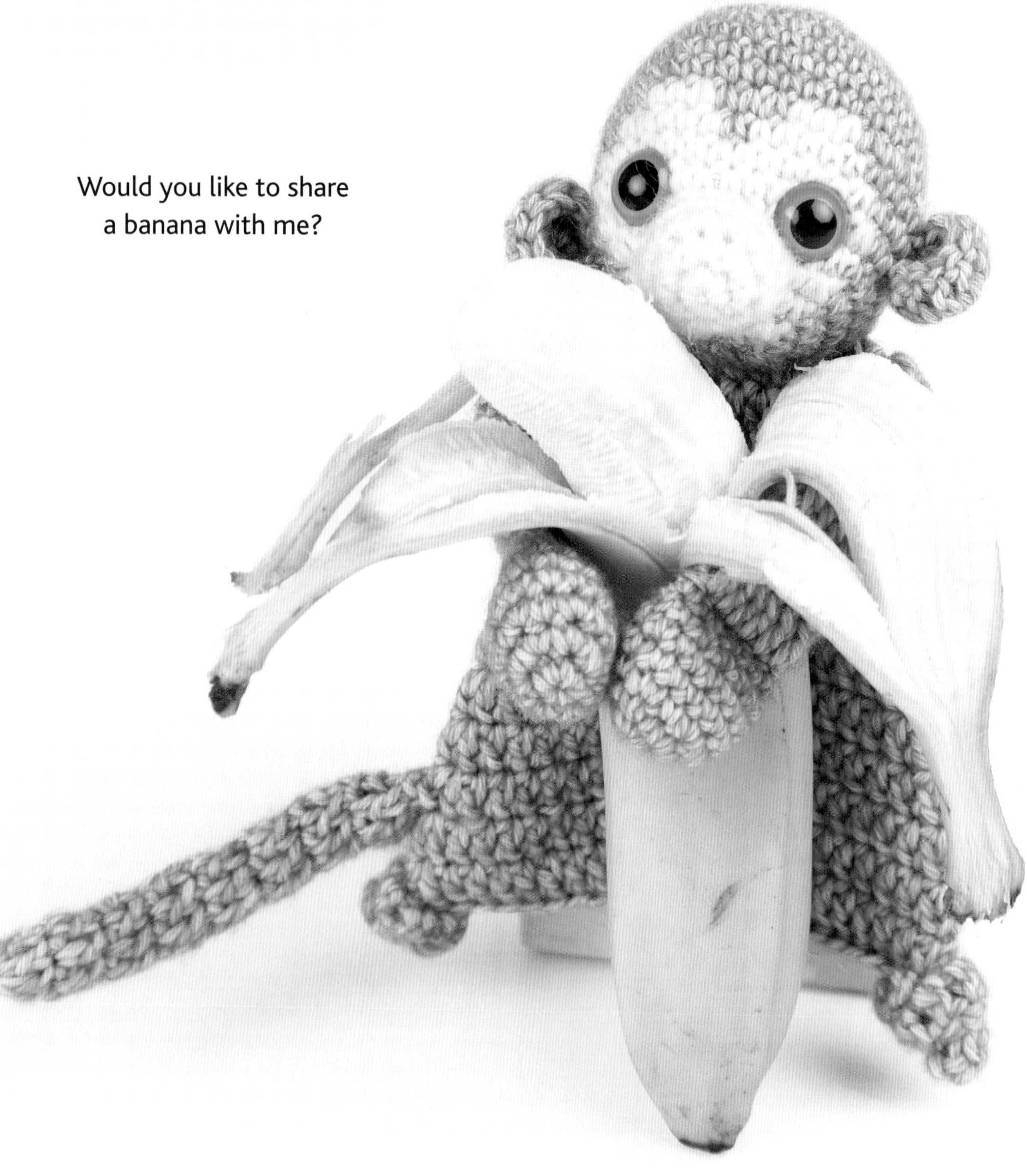

DIMENSIONS

5.9 in. (15 cm) long and 3.9 in. (10 cm) wide

MATERIALS

DK #3 lightweight yarn (sample shown in Scheepjes Stone Washed):
- beige (Boulder Opal): 109.4 yd. (100 m)
- light pink (Pink Quartzite): 76.6 yd. (70 m)

Crochet hook: US size D-3 (3 mm)
Black and blue safety eyes, 12 mm
Fiberfill stuffing
Yarn needle and scissors

DIFFICULTY LEVEL

HEAD

Rnd 1: With beige, start with a magic ring, 6sc in the ring. (6)
Rnd 2: 2sc in each stitch around. (12)
Rnd 3: *Sc1, 2sc in next*, repeat from * to * around. (18)
Rnd 4: *Sc2, 2sc in next*, repeat from * to * around. (24)
Rnd 5: *Sc3, 2sc in next*, repeat from * to * around. (30)
Rnd 6: *Sc4, 2sc in next*, repeat from * to * around. (36)
Rnd 7–Rnd 9: Sc1 in each stitch around. (36)
Rnd 10: With beige sc3, **with light pink** sc3, **with beige** sc3, **with light pink** sc3, **with beige** sc24. (36)
Rnd 11: With beige sc2, **with light pink** sc5, **with beige** sc1, **with light pink** sc5, **with beige** sc23. (36)
Rnd 12: With beige sc1, **with light pink** sc13, **with beige** sc22. (36)
Rnd 13: With beige sc1, **with light pink** sc14, **with beige** sc21. (36)
Rnd 14: With beige sc1, **with light pink** sc3, sc2tog, sc4, sc2tog, sc3, **with beige** sc1, sc2tog,*sc4, sc2tog*, repeat from * to * to the end. (30)
Rnd 15: With beige sc1, **with light pink** sc2, *sc2tog, sc3*, repeat from * to * 1 more time, **with beige** sc2tog, *sc3, sc2tog*, repeat from * to * until end. (24)
Rnd 16: With beige sc1, **with light pink** sc1, *sc2tog, sc2*, repeat from * to * 1 more time, sc1, **with beige** sc2tog, sc1, sc2tog, *sc2, sc2tog*, repeat from * to * to end. (18)
At this point, attach the eyes between Rnd 12 and Rnd 13 and fill the head.
Rnd 17: With beige sc1, **with light pink** *sc2tog, sc1*, repeat from * to * 1 more time, sc2tog, **with beige** *sc1, sc2tog*, repeat from * to * until end. (12)
Cut the light pink thread and weave in the ends.
Cut a long piece of beige yarn and close the seam; use the remaining thread to attach the head to the body.

SNOUT

Rnd 1: With light pink, start with a magic ring, 6sc in the ring. (6)
Rnd 2: 2sc in each stitch around. (12)
Rnd 3: *Sc3, 2sc in next*, repeat from * to * around. (15)
Rnd 4: Sc1 in each stitch around. (15)
Cut, leaving a long piece of yarn to secure the snout to the face, making sure that the center is exactly between the eyes, and then sew it to Rnd 14 and Rnd 17 of the head. Secure it three-quarters of the way around, fill it up, and then sew it completely shut.

EARS (MAKE 2)

Rnd 1: With beige, start with a magic ring, 6sc in the ring. (6)
Rnd 2: Sc2, 2dc in each of the 4 following stitches, sl st in first sc. (10)
Cut the yarn, leaving a long thread for securing the ears later.

BODY

Rnd 1: With beige ch13, dc1 in third ch from hook, dc9, 3dc in last, continue along other side of chains, dc10, 3dc in last, sl st in first dc. (26)
Rnd 2: Ch2 (from here on does not count as first stitch), *dc12, 2dc in next*, repeat from * to * 1 more time, sl st in first dc. (28)
Rnd 3: Ch2, *dc13, 2dc in next*, repeat from * to * 1 more time, sl st in first dc. (30)
Rnd 4: Ch2, *dc14, 2dc in next*, repeat from * to * 1 more time, sl st in first dc. (32)
Rnd 5: Ch2, *dc15, 2dc in next*, repeat from * to * 1 more time, sl st in first st. (34)
Rnd 6: Ch2, *dc16, 2dc in next*, repeat from * to * 1 more time , sl st in first st. (36)
Rnd 7: Ch2, *dc17, 2dc in next*, repeat from * to * 1 more time, sl st in first dc. (38)
Rnd 8: Ch2, *dc18, 2dc in next*, repeat from * to * 1 more time, sl st in first dc. (40)
Rnd 9: Ch2, *dc19, 2dc in next*, repeat from * to * 1 more time, sl st in first dc. (42)
Rnd 10: Ch2, *dc20, 2dc in next*, repeat from * to * 1 more time, sl st in first dc. (44)
Rnd 11: Ch2, *dc21, 2dc in next*, repeat from * to * 1 more time, sl st in first dc. (46)
Rnd 12: Ch2, *dc22, ch14, dc1 in 3rd ch from hook, dc1 in each of the 11 remaining stitches, 2dc in next stitch on Rnd 11*, repeat from * to * 1 more time, sl st in first dc.
Cut a long thread to close the body later.

ARMS (MAKE 2)

Rnd 1: With beige, start with a magic ring, 6sc in the ring. (6)
Rnd 2: 2sc in each stitch around. (12)
Rnd 3: *Sc1, 2sc in next*, repeat from * to * around. (18)
Rnd 4–Rnd 5: Sc1 in each stitch around. (18)
Rnd 6: *Sc1, sc2tog*, repeat from * to * around. (12)
Rnd 7: Sc1 in each stitch around. (12)
Rnd 8: Sl st, ch2 (does not count as first dc from now on), dc1 in each stitch around, sl st in first dc. (12)
Rnd 9: Ch2, dc2tog, dc1 in each stitch around, sl st in first dc. (11)
Now fill up the hand, and then take a piece of yarn and sew along the hand between Rnd 7 and Rnd 8.
Rnd 10: Ch2, dc1 in each stitch around, sl st in first dc. (11)
Rnd 11: Ch2, dc2tog, dc1 in each stitch around, sl st in first dc. (10)
Rnd 12: Ch2, dc1 in each stitch around, sl st in first dc. (10)
Rnd 13: Ch2, dc2tog, dc1 in each stitch around, sl st in first dc. (9)
Cut a long thread for securing the arms later.

TAIL

Rnd 1: With beige, start with a magic ring, ch2 (does not count as the first st for the entire pattern), 6dc in the ring, sl st in first dc. (6)
Rnd 2–Rnd 8: Ch2, dc1 in each stitch around, sl st in first dc. (6)
Cut a long thread to secure the tail later.

PUTTING IT ALL TOGETHER

- Sew the 2 sc from Rnd 2 of an ear to each side of the head between Rnd 12 and Rnd 13.
- Fold the body along the increase lines and use the long yarn left on the body to close the bottom.
- Make a knot in the corners to make the feet.
- Sew an arm on each side of the body between Rnd 1 and Rnd 2.
- Sew the tail against the side of the body at Rnd 11.
- Take the head and sew Rnd 14 onto Rnd 1 of the body.

Come and hang out with this wise owl.

DIMENSIONS

11.8 in. (30 cm) long and 6.3 in. (16 cm) wide

MATERIALS

DK #3 lightweight yarn (sample shown in Scheepjes Stone Washed):
- white (Moon Stone): 65.6 yd. (60 m)
- beige (Boulder Opal): 142.2 yd. (130 m)
- brown (Brown Agate): 87.5 yd. (80 m)
- orange (Coral): 54.7 yd. (50 m)

Crochet hook: US size D-3 (3 mm)
Gold and black safety eyes, 15 mm
Fiberfill stuffing
Yarn needle and scissors

SPECIAL STITCH

Feather = skip 1 dc, 2dc in next stitch

DIFFICULTY LEVEL

EYES (MAKE 2)

Rnd 1: With white, start with a magic ring, ch2 (doesn't count as first dc now and throughout), dc12 in the loop, sl st 1 in first dc. (12) Don't pull the ring tight, but leave a little hole to insert the eye.

LEFT EYE

Rnd 2: With brown ch1, 2sc in same stitch as ch1, hdc1, (in next stitch: dc3, ch3, sl st in first of 3 ch, 1tr).

RIGHT EYE

Rnd 2: With brown ch6, sl st in fourth ch from hook, dc3 in same stitch as ch6, hdc1, 2sc in next stitch, sl st in same as 2sc.

FOR BOTH EYES

Cut the white and brown yarn to attach the eyes later.

BEAK

Rnd 1: With orange, start with a magic ring. In the ring: ch1, sc1, hdc1, dc1, tr1, dc1, hdc1, sc1, sl st in first sc. Cut the yarn, but leave a long end to sew the beak on later.

HEAD

Rnd 1: With beige, start with a magic ring, sc6 in the ring. (6)
Rnd 2: Sc2 in each stitch around. (12)
Rnd 3: *Sc1, sc2 in next*, repeat from * to * around. (18)
Rnd 4: *Sc2, sc2 in next*, repeat from * to * around. (24)
Rnd 5: *Sc3, sc2 in next*, repeat from * to * around. (30)
Rnd 6: *Sc4, sc2 in next*, repeat from * to * around. (36)
Rnd 7: *Sc5, sc2 in next*, repeat from * to * around. (42)
Rnd 8: *Sc6, sc2 in next*, repeat from * to * around. (48)
Rnd 9: *Sc7, sc2 in next*, repeat from * to * around. (54)
Rnd 10–Rnd 25: Sc1 in each stitch around. (54)
Rnd 26: *Sc7, sc2tog*, repeat from * to * around. (48)
Rnd 27: *Sc6, sc2tog*, repeat from * to * around. (42)
Rnd 28: In back loops only, *sc5, sc2tog*, repeat from * to * around. (36)

Cut a long thread to close the seam of the head later.
Edge: With beige, attach the yarn in the first unworked front loop of Rnd 27, ch1, sc1 in same stitch as ch1, *skip 2, 7dc in next stitch, skip 2, sc1 in next*, repeat from * to * around, sl st in first sc, cut the yarn and weave in ends.
Take the eyes you've just made and insert the safety eyes between Rnd 18 and Rnd 19 (with 5 stitches in between, counted from the white edge) through the head and attach the back of each safety eye inside the head (make extra sure they're firmly attached, since it's a bit harder to attach the back through two layers).
Sew the edges to the head (white part with remaining white yarn and brown piece with the remaining brown yarn).
Sew the beak in the center between the eyes in Rnd 20–Rnd 24.
Stuff the head with fiberfill and close the seam with the remaining yarn.

BODY

Rnd 1: With brown ch18, 1dc in third ch from hook, dc14, 3dc in last, continue along other side of chains, dc15, 3dc in last, sl st in first dc. (36)
Rnd 2: With brown ch2 (doesn't count as first dc now and throughout), dc3, ***with white** feather, **with brown** feather*, repeat from * to * 1 more time, **with white** feather, **with brown** dc4, 2dc in next stitch, dc17, 2dc in next, sl st in first dc. (38)
Rnd 3: With brown ch2, dc5, ***with white** feather, **with brown** feather*, repeat from * to * 1 more time, **with white** feather, **with brown** dc3, 2dc in next stitch, dc18, 2dc in next, sl st in first dc. (40)
Rnd 4: With brown ch2, dc3, ***with white** feather, **with brown** feather*, repeat from * to * 2 more times, **with white** feather, **with brown** dc2, 2dc in next stitch, dc19, 2dc in next, sl st in first dc. (42)
Rnd 5: With brown ch2, dc5, ***with white** feather, **with brown** feather*, repeat from * to * 1 more time, **with white** feather, **with brown** dc5, 2dc in next stitch, dc20, 2dc in next, sl st in first dc. (44)
Rnd 6: With brown ch2, dc3, ***with white** feather, **with brown** feather*, repeat from * to * 2 more times, **with white** feather, **with brown** dc4, 2dc in next stitch, dc21, 2dc in next, sl st in first dc. (46)
Rnd 7: With brown ch2, dc5, ***with white** feather, **with brown** feather*, repeat from * to * 2 more times, **with white** feather, **with brown** dc3, 2dc in next stitch, dc22, 2dc in next, sl st in first dc. (48)
Rnd 8: With brown ch2, dc3, ***with white** feather, **with brown** feather*, repeat from * to * 2 more times, **with white** feather, **with brown** dc6, 2dc in next stitch, dc23, 2dc in next, sl st in first dc. (50)
Rnd 9: With brown ch2, dc5, ***with white** feather, **with brown** feather*, repeat from * to * 2 more times, **with white** feather, **with brown** dc5, 2dc in next stitch, dc24, 2dc in next, sl st in first dc. (52)
Rnd 10: With brown ch2, dc3, ***with white** feather, **with brown** feather*, repeat from * to * 3 more times, **with white** feather, **with brown** dc4, 2dc in next stitch, dc25, 2dc in next, sl st in first dc. (54)
Rnd 11: With brown ch2, dc5, ***with white** feather, **with brown** feather*, repeat from * to * 2 more times, **with white** feather, **with brown** dc7, 2dc in next stitch, dc26, 2dc in next, sl st in first dc. (56)
Rnd 12: With brown ch2, dc3, ***with white** feather, **with brown** feather*, repeat from * to * 3 more times, **with white** feather, **with brown** dc6, 2dc in next stitch, dc27, 2dc in next, sl st in first dc. (58)
Rnd 13: With brown ch2, dc5, ***with white** feather, **with brown** feather*, repeat from * to * 3 more times, **with white** feather, **with brown** dc5, 2dc in next stitch, dc28, 2dc in next, sl st in first dc. (60)
Rnd 14: With brown ch2, dc3, ***with white** feather, **with brown** feather*, repeat from * to * 3 more times, **with white** feather, **with brown** dc8, 2dc in next stitch, dc29, 2dc in next, sl st in first dc. (62)
Rnd 15: With brown ch2, dc5, ***with white** feather, **with brown** feather*, repeat from * to * 3 more times, **with white** feather, **with brown** dc7, 2dc in next stitch, dc30, 2dc in next, sl st in first dc. (64)
Rnd 16: With brown ch2, dc3, ***with white** feather, **with brown** feather*, repeat from * to * 4 more times, **with white** feather, **with brown** dc6, 2dc in next stitch, dc31, 2dc in next, sl st in first dc. (66)
Rnd 17: With brown ch2, dc5, ***with white** feather, **with brown** feather*, repeat from * to * 3 more times, **with white** feather, **with brown** dc9, 2dc in next stitch, dc32, 2dc in next, sl st in first dc. (68)
Rnd 18: With brown ch2, dc3, ***with white** feather, **with brown** feather*, repeat from to * 4 more times, **with white** feather, **with brown** dc8, 2dc in next stitch, dc33, 2dc in next, sl st in first dc. (70)
Rnd 19: With brown ch2, dc5, ***with white** feather, **with brown** feather*, repeat from to * 4 more times, **with white** feather, **with brown** dc7, 2dc in next stitch, dc34, 2dc in next, sl st in first dc. (72)
You can cut the white yarn.
Rnd 20: With brown ch2, *dc35, 2dc in next*, repeat from * to * one more time, sl st in first dc. (74)
Cut the yarn, but leave a long end to close the body in the end; fold the body in line with the increases to make the belly straight.

WINGS (MAKE 2)

Rnd 1: With beige, start with a magic ring, ch2 (doesn't count as first dc now and throughout), 6dc in the ring, sl st in first dc. (6)
Rnd 2: Ch2, 2dc in each stitch around, sl st in first dc. (12)
Rnd 3: Ch2, *dc1, 2dc in next*, repeat from * to * around, sl st in first dc. (18)
Rnd 4: Ch2, *dc2, 2dc in next*, repeat from * to * around, sl st in first dc. (24)
Rnd 5: Ch2, *dc3, 2dc in next*, repeat from * to * around, sl st in first dc. (30)
Rnd 6: Ch2, dc1 in each stitch around, sl st in first dc. (30)
Rnd 7: Ch2, dc2tog twice, dc26, sl st in first dc. (28)
Rnd 8: Ch2, dc2tog twice, dc24, sl st in first dc. (26)
Rnd 9: Ch2, dc2tog twice, dc22, sl st in first dc. (24)
Rnd 10: Ch2, dc2tog twice, dc20, sl st in first dc. (22)
Rnd 11: Ch2, dc2tog twice, dc18, sl st in first dc. (20)
Rnd 12: Ch2, dc2tog twice, dc16, sl st in first dc. (18)
Rnd 13: Ch2, dc2tog twice, dc14, sl st in first dc. (16)
Rnd 14: Ch2, dc2tog twice, dc12, sl st in first dc. (14)
Rnd 15: Ch2, dc2tog twice, dc10, sl st in first dc. (12)
Cut the yarn but leave a long tail to attach the wings in the end.

FEET (MAKE 2)

Rnd 1: With orange, start with a magic ring, 6sc in the ring. (6)
Rnd 2: 2sc in each stitch around. (12)
Rnd 3: *Sc1, 2sc in next*, repeat from * to * around. (18)
Rnd 4: *Sc2, 2sc in next*, repeat from * to * around. (24)
Rnd 5–Rnd 11: Sc1 in each stitch around. (24)
Rnd 12: *Sc1, (in next: 1hdc, 1dc, 1tr, 1dc, 1hdc), sc1, sl st 1*, repeat from * to * around. You'll have three toes (6 repeats).
Cut the yarn but leave a long tail to close the feet in the end.

EARS (MAKE 2)

Rnd 1: With beige, start with a magic ring, ch2 (doesn't count as first dc now and throughout), dc12 in the ring, sl st in first dc. (12)
Rnd 2: Ch2, dc1 in each stitch around, sl st in first dc. (12)
Cut the yarn but leave a long tail to sew on the ears in the end.

PUTTING IT ALL TOGETHER

- Sew an ear to each side of the head in Rnd 8.
- Place both feet between the bottom two layers of the body. With the remaining yarn from the body, sew across the seam with the parts in between. This way you close the bottom and assemble the pieces at the same time.
- Stuff the feet lightly. With the remaining yarn, close the seam of the toes by sewing through both layers.
- Sew a wing to each side of the body between Rnd 2 and Rnd 4.
- Finally, sew Rnd 28 of the head to Rnd 1 of the body.

OWLET

Do you want to dive into an adventure with this little owlet?

DIMENSIONS

8.3 in. (21 cm) long and 3.9 in. (10 cm) wide

MATERIALS

DK #3 lightweight yarn (sample shown in Scheepjes Stone Washed):
- white (Moon Stone): 142.2 yd. (130 m)
- beige (Boulder Opal): 76.6 yd. (70 m)
- orange (Coral): 32.8 yd. (30 m)

Crochet hook: US size D-3 (3 mm)
Gold and black safety eyes, 12 mm
Fiberfill stuffing
Yarn needle and scissors

SPECIAL STITCH

Feather = skip 1 dc, 2dc in next stitch

DIFFICULTY LEVEL

EYES (MAKE 2)

Rnd 1: With white, start with a magic ring, 8sc in the ring. (8) Do not overtighten the ring, but leave a hole to insert the eye.

LEFT EYE

Rnd 2: With beige ch1, 2sc in the same stitch as ch, hdc1, (in next stitch: 2dc, ch3, sl st in first of ch3, 1tr).

RIGHT EYE

Rnd 2: With beige ch6, sl st in fourth ch from your hook, 2dc in the same stitch as the ch6, 1hdc, 2sc in the next stitch, sl st in same as 2sc.

FOR BOTH EYES

Cut yarn, leaving long white and beige threads to secure the eyes later.

BEAK

Rnd 1: With orange, start with a magic ring, ch1, 1sc, 1hdc, 1dc, 1tr, 1dc, 1hdc, 1sc, sl st in first sc. (7)
Cut a long thread to secure the beak later.

HEAD

Rnd 1: With white, start with a magic ring, 6sc in the ring. (6)
Rnd 2: 2sc in each sc around. (12)
Rnd 3: *Sc1, 2sc in next*, repeat from * to * around. (18)
Rnd 4: *Sc2, 2sc in next*, repeat from * to * around. (24)
Rnd 5: *Sc3, 2sc in next*, repeat from * to * around. (30)
Rnd 6: *Sc4, 2sc in next*, repeat from * to * around. (36)
Rnd 7: *Sc5, 2sc in next*, repeat from * to * around. (42)
Rnd 8–Rnd 20: Sc1 in each sc around. (42)
Rnd 21: In back loops only, *Sc5, sc2tog*, repeat from * to * around. (36)
Cut a long thread to close the head later.

Edge: With white, attach the thread in the first front loop of Rnd 20 that you have not worked in: ch1, 1sc in same as ch1, *skip 2, 7dc in next, skip 2, sc1 in next*, repeat from * to * around, sl st in first sc.
Cut the thread and weave in the ends.
Take the eyes that you just hooked and insert the safety eyes between Rnd 13 and Rnd 14 (with 6 stitches in between, counted from the white edge) through the head, and attach the back of each safety eye inside the head (check carefully to confirm that they are secure, as it is more difficult to pass them through two layers). Now sew on using the remaining threads of the eye (white piece with white thread and beige piece with beige thread).
Sew the beak between the eyes on Rnd 13–Rnd 18.
Fill the head and close the bottom seam.

BODY

Rnd 1: With white ch13, dc1 in third ch from hook, dc9, 3dc in last, continue along other side of chains, dc10, 3dc in last, sl st in first st. (26)
Rnd 2: With white ch2 (does not count as the first dc for the entire pattern), dc2, **with beige** feather (see Special Stitch on page 77), **with white** feather, **with beige** feather, **with white** dc4, 2dc in next stitch, dc12, 2dc in next, sl st in first dc. (28)
Rnd 3: With white ch2, dc4, **with beige** feather, **with white** feather, **with beige** feather, **with white** dc3, 2dc in next stitch, dc13, 2dc in next, sl st in first dc. (30)
Rnd 4: With white ch2, dc2, ***with beige** feather, **with white** feather *, repeat from * to * 1 more time, **with beige** feather, **with white** dc2, 2dc in next stitch, dc14, 2dc in next, sl st in first dc. (32)
Rnd 5: With white ch2, dc4, **with beige** feather, **with white** feather, **with beige** feather, **with white** dc5, 2dc in next stitch, dc15, 2dc in next, sl st in first dc. (34)
Rnd 6: With white ch2, dc2; ***with beige** feather, **with white** feather *, repeat from * to * 1 more time, **with beige** feather, **with white** dc4, 2dc in next stitch, dc16, 2dc in next, sl st in first dc. (36)
Rnd 7: With white ch2, dc4, * **with beige** feather, **with white** feather*, repeat from * to * 1 more time, **with beige** feather, **with white** dc3, 2dc in next stitch, dc17, 2dc in next, sl st in first dc. (38)
Rnd 8: With white ch2, dc2, ***with beige** feather, **with white** feather*, repeat from * to * 1 more time, **with beige** feather, **with white** dc6, 2dc in next stitch, dc18, 2dc in next, sl st in first dc. (40)
Rnd 9: With white ch2, dc4, ***with beige** feather, **with white** feather*, repeat from * to * 1 more time, **with beige** feather, **with white** dc5, 2dc in next stitch, dc19, 2dc in next, sl st in first dc. (42)
Rnd 10: With white ch2, dc2; ***with beige** feather, **with white** feather*, repeat from * to * 2 more times, **with beige** feather, **with white** dc4, 2dc in next stitch, dc20, 2dc in next, sl st in first dc. (44)
Rnd 11: With white ch2, dc4, ***with beige** feather, **with white** feather*, repeat from * to * 1 more time, **with beige** feather, **with white** dc7, 2dc in next stitch, dc21, 2dc in next, sl st in first dc. (46)
Rnd 12: With white ch2, dc2, ***with beige** feather, **with white** feather*, repeat from * to * 2 more times, **with beige** feather, **with white** dc6, 2dc in next stitch, dc22, 2dc in next, sl st in first dc. (48)
Rnd 13: With white ch2, dc4, ***with beige** feather, **with white** feather*, repeat from * to * 2 more times, **with beige** feather, **with white** dc5, 2dc in next stitch, dc23, 2dc in next, sl st in first dc. (50)
You can cut the beige thread.
Rnd 14: With white ch2, *dc24, 2dc in next*, repeat from * to * 1 more time, sl st in first dc. (52)
Cut a long thread to close the body at the end, fold the body on the line of the increases.

WINGS (MAKE 2)

Rnd 1: With beige, start with a magic ring, ch2 (does not count as the first dc for the entire pattern), 6dc in the ring, sl st in first dc. (6)
Rnd 2: Ch2, 2dc in every stitch around, sl st in first dc. (12)
Rnd 3: Ch2, *dc1, 2dc in next*, repeat from * to * around, sl st in first dc. (18)
Rnd 4: Ch2, *dc2, 2dc in next*, repeat from * to * around, sl st in first dc. (24)
Rnd 5: Ch2, dc1 in each stitch around, sl st in first dc. (24)
Rnd 6: Ch2, dc2tog 3 times, dc18, sl st in first dc. (21)
Rnd 7: Ch2, dc2tog 3 times, dc15, sl st in first dc. (18)
Rnd 8: Ch2, dc2tog 3 times, dc12, sl st in first dc. (15)
Rnd 9: Ch2, dc2tog 3 times, dc9, sl st in first dc. (12)
Rnd 10: Ch2, dc2tog 3 times, dc6, sl st in first dc. (9)
Cut a long thread to secure the wings later.

FEET (MAKE 2)

Rnd 1: With orange, start with a magic ring, 6sc in the ring. (6)
Rnd 2: 2sc in each stitch around. (12)
Rnd 3: *Sc1, 2sc in next*, repeat from * to * around. (18)
Rnd 4–Rnd 5: Sc1 in each stitch around. (18)
Rnd 6: *Sc1, (in next stitch: 1hdc, 1dc, 1tr, 1dc, 1hdc), sl st*, repeat from * to * all around. You will have three toes (6 repeats).
Cut the yarn but leave a long tail to close the feet in the end.

EARS (MAKE 2)

Rnd 1: With beige, start with a magic ring, ch2 (does not count as first dc for the entire pattern), 8dc in the ring, sl st in first dc. (8)
Rnd 2: Ch2, dc1 in each stitch around, sl st in first dc. (8)
Cut a long thread for securing the ears later.

PUTTING IT ALL TOGETHER

- Sew on the ears against Rnd 8 of the head.
- Place each foot between the two layers at the bottom of the body, and then use the remaining yarn to sew along the bottom with the two feet in between, closing the seam and attaching the parts at the same time.
- Fill the feet lightly. With the remaining yarn, sew each foot tightly through both layers of the toes.
- Sew a wing on each side of the body between Rnd 1 and Rnd 3.
- Sew Rnd 21 of the head onto Rnd 1 of the body.

PENGUIN

I'm trying a new way of fishing. Would you like to join me?

DIMENSIONS

11 in. (28 cm) long and 7.1 in. (18 cm) wide

MATERIALS

DK #3 lightweight yarn (sample shown in Scheepjes Stone Washed):

- gray (Smokey Quartz): 164 yd. (150 m)
- white (Moon Stone): 109.4 yd. (100 m)
- orange (Coral): 54.7 yd. (50 m)

Crochet hook: US size D-3 (3 mm)
Black safety eyes, 12 mm
Small amount of fiberfill stuffing
Yarn needle and scissors

DIFFICULTY LEVEL

HEAD

Rnd 1: With gray, start with a magic ring, 6sc in the ring. (6)
Rnd 2: 2sc in each stitch around. (12)
Rnd 3: *Sc1, 2sc in next*, repeat from * to * around. (18)
Rnd 4: *Sc2, 2sc in next*, repeat from * to * around. (24)
Rnd 5: *Sc3, 2sc in next*, repeat from * to * around. (30)
Rnd 6: *Sc4, 2sc in next*, repeat from * to * around. (36)
Rnd 7: *Sc5, 2sc in next*, repeat from * to * around. (42)
Rnd 8: *Sc6, 2sc in next*, repeat from * to * around. (48)
Rnd 9: *Sc7, 2sc in next*, repeat from * to * around. (54)
Rnd 10–Rnd 14: Sc1 in each stitch around. (54)
Rnd 15: Sc6, **with white** sc3, **with gray** sc9, **with white** sc3, **with gray** sc33. (54)
Rnd 16: Sc5, **with white** sc5, **with gray** sc7, **with white** sc5, **with gray** sc32. (54)
Rnd 17: Sc4, **with white** sc7, **with gray** sc5, **with white** sc7, **with gray** sc31. (54)
Rnd 18: Sc3, **with white** sc9, **with gray** sc3, **with white** sc9, **with gray** sc30. (54)
Rnd 19: Sc3, **with white** sc10, **with gray** sc1, **with white** sc11, **with gray** sc29. (54)
Rnd 20: Sc3, **with white** sc23, **with gray** sc28. (54)
Rnd 21: Sc2tog, sc1, **with white** sc6, sc2tog, sc7, sc2tog, sc6, **with gray** sc1, *sc2tog, sc7* repeat from * to * to end. (48)
Rnd 22: Sc2tog, sc1, **with white** sc5, sc2tog, sc6, sc2tog, sc5, **with gray** sc1, *sc2tog, sc6*, repeat from * to * to end. (42)
Rnd 23: Sc2tog, sc1, **with white** sc4, sc2tog, sc5, sc2tog, sc4, **with gray** sc1, *sc2tog, sc5*, repeat from * to * to end. (36)
Rnd 24: Sc2tog, sc1, **with white** sc3, sc2tog, sc4, sc2tog, sc3, **with gray** sc1, *sc2tog, sc4*, repeat from * to * to end. (30)
Rnd 25: Sc2tog, sc1, **with white** sc2, sc2tog, sc3, sc2tog, sc2, **with gray** sc1, *sc2tog, sc3*, repeat from * to * to end. (24)

Rnd 26: Sc2tog, sc1, **with white** sc1, sc2tog, sc2, sc2tog, sc1, **with gray** sc1, *sc2tog, sc2*, repeat from * to * to end. (18)

At this point, attach safety eyes between Rnd 19 and Rnd 20 and stuff the head.

Rnd 27: Sc2tog, sc1, **with white** sc2tog, sc1, sc2tog, **with gray** sc1, *sc2tog, sc1*, repeat from * to * to end. (12)

Cut a long tail and sew the seam closed.

BODY

Rnd 1: With gray ch20, dc in third ch from hook, dc16, 3dc in last, continue along other side of chains, dc17, 3dc in last, sl st in first dc. (40)

Rnd 2: Ch2 (doesn't count as first stitch for entire pattern), *dc19, 2dc in next*, repeat from * to * one more time, sl st in first dc. (42)

Rnd 3: Ch2, *dc20, 2dc in next*, repeat from * to * one more time, sl st in first dc. (44)

Rnd 4: Ch2, *dc21, 2dc in next*, repeat from * to * one more time, sl st in first dc. (46)

Rnd 5: Ch2, *dc22, 2dc in next*, repeat from * to * one more time, sl st in first dc. (48)

Rnd 6: Ch2, *dc23, 2dc in next*, repeat from * to * one more time, sl st in first dc. (50)

Rnd 7: Ch2, *dc24, 2dc in next*, repeat from * to * one more time, sl st in first dc. (52)

Rnd 8: Ch2, *dc25, 2dc in next*, repeat from * to * one more time, sl st in first dc. (54)

Rnd 9: Ch2, *dc26, 2dc in next*, repeat from * to * one more time, sl st in first dc. (56)

Rnd 10: Ch2, dc3, **with white** dc19, **with gray** dc5, 2dc in next, dc27, 2dc in next, sl st in first dc. (58)

Rnd 11: Ch2, dc3, **with white** dc20, **with gray** dc5, 2dc in next, dc28, 2dc in next, sl st in first dc. (60)

Rnd 12: Ch2, dc3, **with white** dc21, **with gray** dc5, 2dc in next, dc29, 2dc in next, sl st in first dc. (62)

Rnd 13: Ch2, dc3, **with white** dc22, **with gray** dc5, 2dc in next, dc30, 2dc in next, sl st in first dc. (64)

Rnd 14: Ch2, dc3, **with white** dc23, **with gray** dc5, 2dc in next, dc31, 2dc in next, sl st in first dc. (66)

Rnd 15: Ch2, dc3, **with white** dc24, **with gray** dc5, 2dc in next, dc32, 2dc in next, sl st in first dc. (68)

Rnd 16: Ch2, dc3, **with white** dc25, **with gray** dc5, 2dc in next, dc33, 2dc in next, sl st in first dc. (70)

Rnd 17: Ch2, dc3, **with white** dc26, **with gray** dc5, 2dc in next, dc34, 2dc in next, sl st in first dc. (72)

Rnd 18: Ch2, dc3, **with white** dc27, **with gray** dc5, 2dc in next, dc35, 2dc in next, sl st in first dc. (74)

Rnd 19: Ch2, dc3, **with white** dc28, **with gray** dc5, 2dc in next, dc36, 2dc in next, sl st in first dc. (76)

Rnd 20: Ch2, dc3, **with white** dc29, **with gray** dc5, 2dc in next, dc37, 2dc in next, sl st in first dc. (78)

Cut a long tail to close body and attach feet in the end.

FEET (MAKE 2)

Rnd 1: With orange, start with a magic ring, 6sc in the ring. (6)

Rnd 2: 2sc in each stitch around. (12)

Rnd 3: *Sc1, 2sc in next*, repeat from * to * around. (18)

Rnd 4: *Sc2, 2sc in next*, repeat from * to * around. (24)

Rnd 5–Rnd 11: Sc1 in each stitch around. (24)

Rnd 12: *Sc1, (in next: hdc1, dc1, tr1, dc1, hdc1), sc1, sl st 1*, repeat around. You'll end up with three toes (6 repeats).

Cut a long tail to close the seam of the feet in the end.

WINGS (MAKE 2)

Rnd 1: With gray, start with a magic ring, ch2, 6dc in the ring, sl st in first dc. (6)

Rnd 2: Ch2, 2dc in each stitch around, sl st in first dc. (12)

Rnd 3: Ch2, *dc1, 2dc in next*, repeat from * to * around, sl st in first dc. (18)

Rnd 4: Ch2, *dc2, 2dc in next*, repeat from * to * around, sl st in first dc. (24)

Rnd 5: Ch2, dc1 in each stitch around, sl st in first dc. (24)

Rnd 6: Ch2, *dc2, dc2tog*, repeat from * to * two more times (3 decreases in total), dc12, sl st in first dc. (21)

Rnd 7: Ch2, dc1 in each stitch around, sl st in first dc. (21)

Rnd 8: Ch2, *dc1, dc2tog* repeat two more times (3 decreases in total), dc12, sl st in first dc. (18)

Rnd 9: Ch2, dc1 in each stitch around, sl st in first dc. (18)

Rnd 10: Ch2, dc2tog three times (3 decreases in total), dc12, sl st in first dc. (15)

Rnd 11: Ch2, dc1 in each stitch around, sl st in first dc. (15)

Cut a long tail to attach wings in the end.

BEAK

Rnd 1: With orange, start with a magic ring, 6sc in the ring. (6)

Rnd 2: 2sc in each stitch around. (12)

Rnd 3: *Sc1, 2sc in next*, repeat from * to * around. (18)

Rnd 4–Rnd 5: Sc1 in each stitch around. (18)

Cut a long tail to attach beak in the end.

PUTTING IT ALL TOGETHER

- Place each foot between the bottom two layers of the body; take the remaining yarn from the body and sew across the seam, with the feet in between, to close and at the same time attach the feet.
- Stuff the feet lightly. With the remaining yarn, sew each foot closed, going through both layers of toes.
- Stuff the beak lightly and sew to the head; leave 1 row of white between the beak and the gray point of head.
- Sew Rnd 21 of the head to Rnd 1 of the body.
- Finally, sew a wing to each side of the body as shown in photo.

BABY PENGUIN

Welcome this baby with open arms.

DIMENSIONS

7.1 in. (18 cm) long and 3.9 in. (10 cm) wide

MATERIALS

DK #3 lightweight yarn (sample shown in Scheepjes Stone Washed):
- gray (Smokey Quartz): 142.2 yd. (130 m)
- white (Moon Stone): 76.6 yd. (70 m)
- orange (Coral): 54.7 yd. (50 m)

Crochet hook: US D-3 (3 mm)
Black and blue safety eyes, 12 mm
Small amount of fiberfill stuffing
Yarn needle and scissors

DIFFICULTY LEVEL

HEAD

Rnd 1: With gray, start with a magic ring, 6sc in the ring. (6)
Rnd 2: 2sc in each stitch around. (12)
Rnd 3: *Sc1, 2sc in next*, repeat from * to * around. (18)
Rnd 4: *Sc2, 2sc in next*, repeat from * to * around. (24)
Rnd 5: *Sc3, 2sc in next*, repeat from * to * around. (30)
Rnd 6: *Sc4, 2sc in next*, repeat from * to * around. (36)
Rnd 7–Rnd 9: Sc1 in each stitch around. (36)
Rnd 10: Sc3, **with white** sc3, **with gray** sc3, **with white** sc3, **with gray** sc24. (36)
Rnd 11: Sc2, **with white** sc5, **with gray** sc1, **with white** sc5, **with gray** sc23. (36)
Rnd 12: Sc1, **with white** sc13, **with gray** sc22. (36)
Rnd 13: Sc1, **with white** sc14, **with gray** sc21. (36)
Rnd 14: Sc1, **with white** sc3, sc2tog, sc4, sc2tog, sc3, **with gray** sc1, sc2tog, *sc4, sc2tog*, repeat from * to * to end. (30)
Rnd 15: Sc1, **with white** sc2, *sc2tog, sc3*, repeat from * to * 1 more time, **with gray** sc2tog, *sc3, sc2tog*, repeat from * to * to end. (24)
Rnd 16: Sc1, **with white** sc1, *sc2tog, sc2*, repeat from * to * 1 more time, sc1, **with gray** sc2tog, sc1, sc2tog, *sc2, sc2tog*, repeat from * to * to end. (18)
At this point, attach safety eyes between Rnd 12 and Rnd 13 and stuff the head.
Rnd 17: Sc1, **with white** *sc2tog, sc1*, repeat from * to * one more time, sc2tog, **with gray** *sc1, sc2tog*, repeat from * to * to end. (12)
Cut white yarn and weave it in. Cut a long tail of the gray yarn and sew the seam closed; you can use the remaining yarn to attach head to body later.

BODY

Rnd 1: With gray ch13, 1dc in third ch from hook, dc9, 4dc in last, continue along other side of chains, dc9, 3dc in last, sl st in first dc. (26)
Rnd 2: Ch2 (doesn't count as first stitch for entire pattern) *dc12, 2dc in next*, repeat from * to * one more time, sl st in first dc. (28)
Rnd 3: Ch2, *dc13, 2dc in next*, repeat from * to * one more time, sl st in first dc. (30)
Rnd 4: Ch2, dc3, **with white** dc8, **with gray** dc3, 2dc in next, dc14, 2dc in next, sl st in first dc. (32)
Rnd 5: Ch2, dc3, **with white** dc9, **with gray** dc3, 2dc in next, dc15, 2dc in next, sl st in first dc. (34)
Rnd 6: Ch2, dc3, **with white** dc10, **with gray** dc3, 2dc in next, dc16, 2dc in next, sl st in first dc. (36)
Rnd 7: Ch2, dc3, **with white** dc11, **with gray** dc3, 2dc in next, dc17, 2dc in next, sl st in first dc. (38)
Rnd 8: Ch2, dc3, **with white** dc12, **with gray** dc3, 2dc in next, dc18, 2dc in next, sl st in first dc. (40)
Rnd 9: Ch2, dc3, **with white** dc13, **with gray** dc3, 2dc in next, dc19, 2dc in next, sl st in first dc. (42)

Rnd 10: Ch2, dc3, **with white** dc14, **with gray** dc3, 2dc in next, dc20, 2dc in next, sl st in first dc. (44)
Rnd 11: Ch2, dc3, **with white** dc15, **with gray** dc3, 2dc in next, dc21, 2dc in next, sl st in first dc. (46)
You can cut the white yarn and weave it in.
Rnd 12: Ch2, *dc22, 2dc in next*, repeat from * to * one more time, sl st in first dc. (48)
Cut a long tail to close the body and attach feet at the end, making sure to fold the body on the line of the increases.

FEET (MAKE 2)

Rnd 1: With orange, start with a magic ring, 6sc in the ring. (6)
Rnd 2: 2sc in each stitch around. (12)
Rnd 3: *Sc1, 2sc in next*, repeat from * to * around. (18)
Rnd 4–Rnd 5: Sc1 in each stitch around. (18)
Rnd 6: *Sc1, (in next: hdc1, dc1, tr1, dc1, hdc1), sl st 1*, repeat around. You'll end up with three toes (6 repeats).
Cut a long tail to close the seam of the feet at the end.

WINGS (MAKE 2)

Rnd 1: With gray, start with a magic ring, ch2, 6dc in the ring, sl st in first dc. (6)
Rnd 2: Ch2, 2dc in each stitch around, sl st in first dc. (12)
Rnd 3: Ch2, *dc1, 2dc in next*, repeat from * to * around, sl st in first dc. (18)
Rnd 4: Ch2, dc1 in each stitch around, sl st in first dc. (18)
Rnd 5: Ch2, *dc1, dc2tog*, repeat from * to * two more times (3 decreases in total), dc9, sl st in first dc. (15)
Rnd 6: Ch2, dc1 in each stitch around, sl st in first dc. (15)
Rnd 7: Ch2, dc2tog three times (3 decreases in total), dc9, sl st in first dc. (12)
Rnd 8: Ch2, dc1 in each stitch around, sl st in first dc. (12)
Cut a long tail to attach wings at the end.

BEAK

Rnd 1: With orange, start with a magic ring, 6sc in the ring. (6)
Rnd 2: 2sc in each stitch around. (12)
Rnd 3: Sc1 in each stitch around. (12)
Cut a long tail to attach the beak at the end.

PUTTING IT ALL TOGETHER

- Place the feet between the bottom two layers of the body. Using the remaining yarn from the body, sew across the seam, with the feet in between, closing the body and at the same time attaching the feet.
- Stuff the feet lightly. With the remaining yarn, sew each foot closed going through both layers of toes.
- Stuff the beak very lightly and sew to the head, in between the eyes.
- Sew a wing to each side of the body in Rnd 1–Rnd 3.
- Sew Rnd 14 of the head to Rnd 1 of the body.

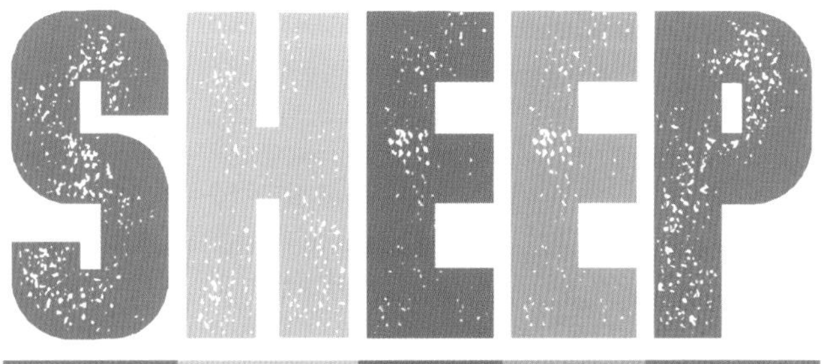

SHEEP

DIMENSIONS

12.6 in. (32 cm) long and 5.9 in. (15 cm) wide

MATERIALS

DK #3 lightweight yarn (sample shown in Scheepjes Stone Washed):
- gray (Smokey Quartz): 196.9 yd. (180 m)
- white (Moon Stone): 87.5 yd. (80 m)

Crochet hook: US D-3 (3 mm)
Black and blue safety eyes, 15 mm
Fiberfill stuffing
Yarn needle and scissors

DIFFICULTY LEVEL

HEAD

Rnd 1: With gray, start with a magic ring, 6sc in the ring. (6)
Rnd 2: 2sc in each stitch around. (12)
Rnd 3: *Dc3tog in 1 stitch, 2sc in next*, repeat from * to * around. (18)
Note: The dc3tog bobbles tend to pop to the inside, so I like to pop them all out with my finger after each round.
Rnd 4: *2sc in next, sc1, dc3tog in 1 stitch*, repeat from * to * around. (24)
Rnd 5: *2sc in next, dc3tog in 1 stitch, sc2*, repeat from * to * around. (30)
Rnd 6: *2sc in next, dc3tog in 1 stitch, sc2, dc3tog in 1 stitch*, repeat from * to * around. (36)
Rnd 7: *2sc in next, dc3tog in 1 stitch, sc2, dc3tog in 1 stitch, sc1*, repeat from * to * around. (42)
Rnd 8: *2sc in next, dc3tog in 1 stitch, sc2, dc3tog in 1 stitch, sc2*, repeat from * to * around. (48)
Rnd 9: *2sc in next, dc3tog in 1 stitch, sc2, dc3tog in 1 stitch, sc2, dc3tog in 1 stitch*, repeat from * to * around. (54)
Rnd 10: *Sc1, dc3tog in next stitch, sc1*, repeat from * to * around. (54)
Rnd 11: *Dc3tog in next stitch, sc2*, repeat from * to * around. (54)
Rnd 12: *Sc2, dc3tog in next stitch*, repeat from * to * around. (54)
Rnd 13–Rnd 15: Repeat Rnd 10–Rnd 12.
Rnd 16–Rnd 30: Continue with white, sc1 in each stitch around. (54)
Rnd 31: *Sc7, sc2tog*, repeat from * to * around. (48)
Rnd 32: *Sc6, sc2tog*, repeat from * to * around. (42)
Rnd 33: *Sc5, sc2tog*, repeat from * to * around. (36)
Rnd 34: *Sc4, sc2tog*, repeat from * to * around. (30)
Rnd 35: *Sc3, sc2tog*, repeat from * to * around. (24)
Rnd 36: *Sc2, sc2tog*, repeat from * to * around. (18)
Now attach the eyes between Rnd 21 and Rnd 22 with 12 stitches between them and stuff the head.
Rnd 37: *Sc1, sc2tog* repeat from * to * around. (12)
Cut yarn, weave through the 12 remaining stitches, pull tight and secure.

EARS (MAKE 2)

Rnd 1: With gray, start with a magic ring, 6sc in the ring. (6)
Rnd 2: 2sc in each stitch around. (12)
Rnd 3: *Sc1, 2sc in next*, repeat from * to * around. (18)
Rnd 4–Rnd 7: Sc1 in each stitch around. (18)
Rnd 8: *Sc1, sc2tog*, repeat from * to * around. (12)
Rnd 9: Sc2tog, sc1 in each stitch around. (11)
Rnd 10: Sc2tog, sc1 in each stitch around. (10)
Rnd 11: Sc2tog, sc1 in each stitch around. (9)
Rnd 12: Sc2tog, sc1 in each stitch around. (8)
Cut yarn but leave a long tail and sew ears to head in Rnd 15.

BODY

Rnd 1: With gray ch18, 1dc in third ch from hook, dc14, 3dc in last, continue along other side of chains, dc15, 3dc in last, sl st in first dc. (36)

Rnd 2: Ch2 (doesn't count as first stitch now and throughout), *dc17, 2dc in next*, repeat from * to * one more time, sl st in first dc. (38)
Rnd 3: Ch2, *dc18, 2dc in next*, repeat from * to * one more time, sl st in first dc. (40)
Rnd 4: Ch2, *dc19, 2dc in next*, repeat from * to * one more time, sl st in first dc. (42)
Rnd 5: Ch2, *dc20, 2dc in next*, repeat from * to * one more time, sl st in first dc. (44)
Rnd 6: Ch2, *dc21, 2dc in next*, repeat from * to * one more time, sl st in first dc. (46)
Rnd 7: Ch2, *dc22, 2dc in next*, repeat from * to * one more time, sl st in first dc. (48)
Rnd 8: Ch2, *dc23, 2dc in next*, repeat from * to * one more time, sl st in first dc. (50)
Rnd 9: Ch2, *dc24, 2dc in next*, repeat from * to * one more time, sl st in first dc. (52)
Rnd 10: Ch2, *dc25, 2dc in next*, repeat from * to * one more time, sl st in first dc. (54)
Rnd 11: Ch2, *dc26, 2dc in next*, repeat from * to * one more time, sl st in first dc. (56)
Rnd 12: Ch2, *dc27, 2dc in next*, repeat from * to * one more time, sl st in first dc. (58)
Rnd 13: Ch2, *dc28, 2dc in next*, repeat from * to * one more time, sl st in first dc. (60)
Rnd 14: Ch2, *dc29, 2dc in next*, repeat from * to * one more time, sl st in first dc. (62)
Rnd 15: Ch2, *dc30, 2dc in next*, repeat from * to * one more time, sl st in first dc. (64)
Rnd 16: Ch2, *dc31, 2dc in next*, repeat from * to * one more time, sl st in first dc. (66)
Rnd 17: Ch2, *dc32, 2dc in next*, repeat from * to * one more time, sl st in first dc. (68)
Rnd 18: Ch2, *dc33, 2dc in next*, repeat from * to * one more time, sl st in first dc. (70)
Rnd 19: Ch2, *dc34, 2dc in next*, repeat from * to * one more time, sl st in first dc. (72)
Cut a long tail to close the body in the end; fold the body in line with the increases to make the belly straight.

ARMS (MAKE 2)

Rnd 1: With gray, start with a magic ring, 6sc in the ring. (6)
Rnd 2: 2sc in each stitch around. (12)
Rnd 3: *Sc1, 2sc in next*, repeat from * to * around. (18)
Rnd 4: *Sc2, 2sc in next*, repeat from * to * around. (24)
Rnd 5–Rnd 9: Sc1 in each stitch around. (24)
Rnd 10: *Sc2, sc2tog*, repeat from * to * around. (18)
Rnd 11–Rnd 12: Sc1 in each stitch around. (18)
Rnd 13: Sl st 1, ch2 (doesn't count as first stitch now and throughout), dc1 in each stitch around, sl st in first dc. (18)
Rnd 14: Ch2, dc2tog, dc1 in each stitch around, sl st in first dc. (17)
At this point, stuff the hand and, with a small piece of the blue yarn, sew across the arm between Rnd 12 and Rnd 13.
Rnd 15: Ch2, dc1 in each stitch around, sl st in first dc. (17)
Rnd 16: Ch2, dc2tog, dc1 in each stitch around, sl st in first dc. (16)
Rnd 17: Ch2, dc1 in each stitch around, sl st in first dc. (16)
Rnd 18: Ch2, dc2tog, dc1 in each stitch around, sl st in first dc. (15)
Rnd 19: Ch2, dc1 in each stitch around, sl st in first dc. (15)
Rnd 20: Ch2, dc2tog, dc1 in each stitch around, sl st in first dc. (14)
Rnd 21: Ch2, dc1 in each stitch around, sl st in first dc. (14)
Rnd 22: Ch2, dc2tog, dc1 in each stitch around, sl st in first dc. (13)
Cut a long tail to attach arms to body later.

LEGS (MAKE 2)

Rnd 1: With gray, start with a magic ring, ch2, 12dc in the ring, sl st in first dc. (12)
Rnd 2: Ch2, *dc1, 2dc in next*, repeat from * to * around, sl st in first dc. (18)
Rnd 3–Rnd 7: Ch2, dc1 in each stitch around, sl st in first dc. (18)
Cut yarn and weave in ends.

PUTTING IT ALL TOGETHER

- Place both legs between the bottom two layers of the body, and, with the remaining yarn from the body, sew across the seam, with the legs in between, to close the body and at the same time attach the legs.
- Sew an arm to each side of the body between Rnd 1 and Rnd 3.
- Sew Rnd 24 of the head (ears not included) to Rnd 1 of the body.

LAMB

Will you be this lamb's friend?

DIMENSIONS

6.7 in. (17 cm) long and 3.9 in. (10 cm) wide

MATERIALS

DK #3 lightweight yarn (sample shown in Scheepjes Stone Washed):
- white (Moon Stone): 54.7 yd. (50 m)
- light gray (Crystal Quartz): 109.4 yd. (100 m)

Crochet hook: US D-3 (3 mm)
Black and blue safety eyes, 12 mm
Fiberfill stuffing
Yarn needle and scissors

DIFFICULTY LEVEL

HEAD

Rnd 1: With gray, start with a magic ring, 6sc in the ring. (6)

Rnd 2: 2sc in each stitch around. (12)
Rnd 3: *Dc3tog in 1 stitch, 2sc in next*, repeat from * to * around. (18)
Note: The dc3tog bobbles tend to pop to the inside, so I like to pop them out with my finger after each round.
Rnd 4: *2sc in next, sc1, dc3tog in 1 stitch*, repeat from * to * around. (24)
Rnd 5: *2sc in next, sc1, dc3tog in 1 stitch, sc1*, repeat from * to * around. (30)
Rnd 6: *2sc in next, dc3tog in 1 stitch, sc2, dc3tog in 1 stitch*, repeat from * to * around. (36)
Rnd 7: *Sc1, dc3tog in next stitch, sc1*, repeat from * to * around. (36)
Rnd 8: *Dc3tog in next stitch, sc2*, repeat from * to * around. (36)
Rnd 9: *Sc2, dc3tog in next stitch*, repeat from * to * around. (36)
Rnd 10–Rnd 17: Continue with white, sc1 in each stitch around. (36)
Rnd 18: *Sc4, sc2tog*, repeat from * to * around. (30)
Rnd 19: *Sc3, sc2tog*, repeat from * to * around. (24)
Rnd 20: *Sc2, sc2tog*, repeat from * to * around. (18)
Now attach the eyes between Rnd 12 and Rnd 13 with 7 stitches between them and stuff the head.
Rnd 21: *Sc1, sc2tog*, repeat from * to * around. (12)
Cut the yarn, weave through the 12 remaining stitches, pull tight, and secure, but leave a long tail to attach it to the body later.

EARS (MAKE 2)

Rnd 1: With gray, start with a magic ring, 6sc in the ring. (6)
Rnd 2: 2sc in each stitch around. (12)
Rnd 3–Rnd 4: Sc1 in each stitch around. (12)
Rnd 5: *Sc1, sc2tog*, repeat from * to * around. (8)
Rnd 6–Rnd 9: Sc1 in each stitch around. (8)
Cut yarn but leave a long tail and sew the ears to the head in Rnd 9.

BODY

Rnd 1: With gray ch13, 1dc in 3rd ch from hook, dc9, 3dc in last, continue along other side of chains, dc9, 4dc in last, sl st in first dc. (26)
Rnd 2: Ch2 (doesn't count as first stitch now and throughout), *dc12, 2dc in next*, repeat from * to * one more time, sl st in first dc. (28)
Rnd 3: Ch2, *dc13, 2dc in next*, repeat from * to * one more time, sl st in first dc. (30)
Rnd 4: Ch2, *dc14, 2dc in next*, repeat from * to * one more time, sl st in first dc. (32)
Rnd 5: Ch2, *dc15, 2dc in next*, repeat from * to * one more time, sl st in first dc. (34)
Rnd 6: Ch2, *dc16, 2dc in next*, repeat from * to * one more time, sl st in first dc. (36)
Rnd 7: Ch2, *dc17, 2dc in next*, repeat from * to * one more time, sl st in first dc. (38)
Rnd 8: Ch2, *dc18, 2dc in next*, repeat from * to * one more time, sl st in first dc. (40)
Rnd 9: Ch2, *dc19, 2dc in next*, repeat from * to * one more time, sl st in first dc. (42)
Rnd 10: Ch2, *dc20, 2dc in next*, repeat from * to * one more time, sl st in first dc. (44)
Rnd 11: Ch2, *dc21, 2dc in next*, repeat from * to * one more time, sl st in first dc. (46)
Rnd 12: Ch2, *dc22, ch14, 1dc in third ch from hook, 1dc in each of the 11 remaining chains, 2dc in next stitch of Rnd 11*, repeat from * to * one more time, sl st in first dc.
Cut a long tail to close the body.

ARMS (MAKE 2)

Rnd 1: With gray, start with a magic ring, 6sc in the ring. (6)
Rnd 2: 2sc in each stitch around. (12)
Rnd 3: *Sc1, 2sc in next*, repeat from * to * around. (18)
Rnd 4–Rnd 5: Sc1 in each stitch around. (18)
Rnd 6: *Sc1, sc2tog*, repeat from * to * around. (12)
Rnd 7: Sc1 in each stitch around. (12)
Rnd 8: Sl st 1, ch2 (doesn't count as first stitch now and throughout), dc1 in each stitch around, sl st in first dc. (12)
Rnd 9: Ch2, dc2tog, dc1 in each stitch around, sl st in first dc. (11)
At this point, stuff the hand and use a small piece of the gray yarn to sew across the arm between Rnd 7 and Rnd 8.
Rnd 10: Ch2, dc1 in each stitch around, sl st in first dc. (11)
Rnd 11: Ch2, dc2tog, dc1 in each stitch around, sl st in first dc. (10)
Rnd 12: Ch2, dc1 in each stitch around, sl st in first dc. (10)
Rnd 13: Ch2, dc2tog, dc1 in each stitch around, sl st in first dc. (9)
Cut a long tail for attaching the arms.

PUTTING IT ALL TOGETHER

- Fold the body in line with the increases to make the belly straight and sew closed.
- Tie a knot in the corners to form the feet.
- Sew the back of Rnd 18 of the head to Rnd 1 of the body.
- Sew an arm on each side of the body between Rnd 1 and Rnd 2.

OTHER ANIMALS AND FRIENDS

CALICO CAT

This yarn kitten loves yarn.

DIMENSIONS

14.2 in. (36 cm) long and 7.1 in. (18 cm) high

MATERIALS

DK #3 lightweight yarn (sample shown in Scheepjes Stone Washed):

- black (Black Onyx): 142.2 yd. (130 m)
- white (Moon Stone): 142.2 yd. (130 m)
- yellow (Yellow Jasper): 142.2 yd. (130 m)

Tiny bit of light pink yarn for nose
Crochet hook: US size D-3 (3 mm)
Brown and black safety eyes, 15 mm
Small amount of fiberfill stuffing
Yarn needle and scissors

FIRST EAR

Rnd 1: With yellow, start with a magic ring, 6sc in the ring. (6)
Rnd 2: Sc1 in each stitch around. (6)
Rnd 3: 2sc in each stitch around. (12)
Rnd 4–Rnd 5: Sc1 in each stitch around. (12)
Rnd 6: *Sc1, 2sc in next*, repeat from * to * around. (18)
Rnd 7–Rnd 8: Sc1 in each stitch around. (18)
Cut yarn and weave in ends.

SECOND EAR

Rnd 1: With black, start with a magic ring, 6sc in the ring. (6)
Rnd 2: Sc1 in each stitch around. (6)
Rnd 3: 2sc in each stitch around. (12)
Rnd 4–Rnd 5: Sc1 in each stitch around. (12)
Rnd 6: *Sc1, 2sc in next*, repeat from * to * around. (18)
Rnd 7–Rnd 8: Sc1 in each stitch around. (18)
Don't cut the yarn!

Rnd 1: Continue with the black yarn from the second ear, ch9, **take first ear**, sc in each of the 18 stitches of first ear, sc in each of the 9 chains you just made, sc in each of the 18 stitches of second ear. (54)
Rnd 2: Sc13, **with white** sc9, **with black** sc32. (54)
Rnd 3: Sc11, **with white** sc13, **with black** sc30. (54)
Rnd 4: Sc9, **with white** sc17, **with black** sc28. (54)
Rnd 5: Sc7, **with white** sc21, **with black** sc26. (54)
Rnd 6: Sc6, **with white** sc24, **with black** sc24. (54)
Rnd 7: Sc5, **with white** sc27, **with black** sc22. (54)
Rnd 8: Sc4, **with white** sc30, **with black** sc20. (54)
Rnd 9: Sc3, **with white** sc33, **with black** sc18. (54)
Rnd 10: Sc2, **with white** sc36, **with black** sc16. (54)
Rnd 11: Sc1, **with white** sc39, **with black** sc14. (54)
Rnd 12: With white *sc7, sc2tog*, repeat from * to * 3 more times, sc6, **with black** sc1, sc2tog, sc7, sc2tog. (48)
Rnd 13: With white *sc6, sc2tog*, repeat from * to * 4 more times, **with black** sc6, sc2tog. (42)
Rnd 14: With white *sc5, sc2tog*, repeat from * to * 4 more times, **with black** sc5, sc2tog. (36)
Rnd 15: With white *sc4, sc2tog*, repeat from * to * 4 more times, **with black** sc4, sc2tog. (30)
Rnd 16: With white *sc3, sc2tog*, repeat from * to * 4 more times, **with black** sc3, sc2tog. (24)
Rnd 17: With white *sc2, sc2tog*, repeat from * to * 4 more times, **with black** sc2, sc2tog. (18)
At this point, attach the safety eyes between Rnd 9 and Rnd 10 of head; stuff the head.

Rnd 18: With white *sc1, sc2tog*, repeat from * to * 4 more times, **with black** sc1, sc2tog. (12)

Fold seam flat and sew the front and the back of the head together; weave in ends.

Embroider the nose with light pink yarn at Rnd 12 and Rnd 13, centered between the eyes.

BODY

Rnd 1: With black ch20, dc in third ch from hook, dc16, 3dc in last, continue along other side of chains, dc17, 3dc in last, sl st in first dc. (40)

Rnd 2: Ch2 (doesn't count as first stitch for entire pattern), *dc19, 2dc in next*, repeat from * to * one more time, sl st in first dc. (42)

Rnd 3: Ch2, dc3, **with white** dc12, **with black** dc5, 2dc in next, dc20, 2dc in next, sl st in first dc. (44)

Rnd 4: Ch2, dc3, **with white** dc13, **with black** dc5, 2dc in next, dc21, 2dc in next, sl st in first dc. (46)

Rnd 5: Ch2, dc3, **with white** dc14, **with black** dc5, 2dc in next, dc22, 2dc in next, sl st in first dc. (48)

Rnd 6: Ch2, dc3, **with white** dc15, **with black** dc5, 2dc in next, dc23, 2dc in next, sl st in first dc. (50)

Rnd 7: Ch2, dc3, **with white** dc16, **with black** dc5, 2dc in next, dc24, 2dc in next, sl st in first dc. (52)

Rnd 8: Ch2, dc3, **with white** dc17, **with black** dc5, 2dc in next, dc25, 2dc in next, sl st in first dc. (54)

Rnd 9: Ch2, dc3, **with white** dc18, **with black** dc5, 2dc in next, dc26, 2dc in next, sl st in first dc. (56)

Rnd 10: Ch2, dc3, **with white** dc19, **with black** dc5, 2dc in next, dc27, 2dc in next, sl st in first dc. (58)

Rnd 11: Ch2, dc3, **with white** dc20, **with black** dc5, 2dc in next, dc28, 2dc in next, sl st in first dc. (60)

Rnd 12: Ch2, dc3, **with white** dc21, **with black** dc5, 2dc in next, dc29, 2dc in next, sl st in first dc. (62)

Rnd 13: Ch2, dc4, **with white** dc20, **with black** dc6, 2dc in next, dc30, 2dc in next, sl st in first dc. (64)

Rnd 14: Ch2, dc5, **with white** dc19, **with black** dc7, 2dc in next, dc31, 2dc in next, sl st in first dc. (66)

You can cut the black yarn and weave it in.

Rnd 15: With yellow ch2, dc6, **with white** dc18, **with yellow** dc8, 2dc in next, dc32, 2dc in next, sl st in first dc. (68)

Rnd 16: Ch2, dc7, **with white** dc17, **with yellow** dc9, 2dc in next, dc33, 2dc in next, sl st in first dc. (70)

Rnd 17: Ch2, dc8, **with white** dc16, **with yellow** dc10, 2dc in next, dc34, 2dc in next, sl st in first dc. (72)

Rnd 18: Ch2, dc9, **with white** dc15, **with yellow** dc11, 2dc in next, dc35, 2dc in next, sl st in first dc. (74)

Rnd 19: Ch2, *dc36, 2dc in next*, repeat from * to * one more time, sl st in first dc. (76)

Rnd 20: Ch2, *dc37, 2dc in next*, repeat from * to * one more time, sl st in first dc. (78)

Cut a long tail to close body and attach feet in the end.

ARMS (MAKE 2)

Rnd 1: With white, start with a magic ring, 6sc in the ring. (6)

Rnd 2: 2sc in each stitch around. (12)

Rnd 3: *Sc1, 2sc in next*, repeat from * to * around. (18)

Rnd 4: *Sc2, 2sc in next*, repeat from * to * around. (24)

Rnd 5–Rnd 9: Sc1 in each stitch around. (24)

Rnd 10: *Sc2, sc2tog*, repeat from * to * around. (18)

Rnd 11–Rnd 12: Sc1 in each stitch around. (18)

Cut a long white tail to use after Rnd 14.

Rnd 13: With black sl st 1, ch2, dc1 in each stitch around, sl st in first dc. (18)

Rnd 14: Ch2, dc2tog, dc1 in each stitch around, sl st in first dc. (17)

At this point, stuff the hand (not too much) and sew across the arm between Rnd 12 and Rnd 13.

Rnd 15: Ch2, dc1 in each stitch around, sl st in first dc. (17)

Rnd 16: Ch2, dc2tog, dc1 in each stitch around, sl st in first dc. (16)

Rnd 17: Ch2, dc1 in each stitch around, sl st in first dc. (16)

Rnd 18: Ch2, dc2tog, dc1 in each stitch around, sl st in first dc. (15)

Rnd 19: Ch2, dc1 in each stitch around, sl st in first dc. (15)

Rnd 20: Ch2, dc2tog, dc1 in each stitch around, sl st in first dc. (14)

Rnd 21: Ch2, dc1 in each stitch around, sl st in first dc. (14)

Rnd 22: Ch2, dc2tog, dc1 in each stitch around, sl st in first dc. (13)

Cut a long tail to attach the arms to the body in the end.

LEGS (MAKE 2)

Rnd 1: With white, start with a magic ring, 6sc in the ring. (6)

Rnd 2: 2sc in each stitch around. (12)

Rnd 3: *Sc1, 2sc in next*, repeat from * to * around. (18)

Rnd 4: *Sc2, 2sc in next*, repeat from * to * around. (24)

Rnd 5–Rnd 9: Sc1 in each stitch around. (24)

Rnd 10: *Sc2, sc2tog*, repeat from * to * around. (18)

Rnd 11–Rnd 12: Sc1 in each stitch around. (18)

Cut a long white tail to use after Rnd 14.

Rnd 13: With yellow sl st 1, ch2, dc1 in each stitch around, sl st in first dc. (18)

Rnd 14: Ch2, dc2tog, dc1 in each stitch around, sl st in first dc. (17)

At this point, stuff the foot (not too much) and sew across the leg between Rnd 12 and Rnd 13.

Rnd 15: Ch2, dc1 in each stitch around, sl st in first dc. (17)

Rnd 16: Ch2, dc2tog, dc1 in each stitch around, sl st in first dc. (16)

Rnd 17: Ch2, dc1 in each stitch around, sl st in first dc. (16)

Rnd 18: Ch2, dc2tog, dc1 in each stitch around, sl st in first dc. (15)

Cut the yarn and weave in ends.

TAIL

Rnd 1: With yellow, start with a magic ring, 6sc in the ring. (6)
Rnd 2: 2sc in each stitch around. (12)
Rnd 3–Rnd 30: Sc1 in each stitch around. (12)
Stuff the tail every few rounds while you crochet the tail. Cut the yarn and weave in the ends.

PUTTING IT ALL TOGETHER

- Sew Rnd 14 of the head (not counting ears) to Rnd 1 of the body.
- Place both legs and the tail between the bottom two layers of the body and use the remaining yarn from the body to sew across the seam to close the body and at the same time attach all parts.
- Sew an arm to each side of the body between Rnd 2 and Rnd 4.

ELEPHANT

Join the circus with me!

DIMENSIONS

13.4 in. (34 cm) long and 6.3 in. (16 cm) wide

MATERIALS

DK #3 lightweight yarn (sample shown in Scheepjes Stone Washed):
- blue (Blue Apatite): 284.3 yd. (260 m)

Crochet hook: US size D-3 (3 mm)
Black safety eyes, 12 mm
Fiberfill stuffing
Yarn needle and scissors

DIFFICULTY LEVEL

EARS (MAKE 2)

Rnd 1: Start with a magic ring, 6sc in the ring. (6)
Rnd 2: 2sc in each stitch around. (12)
Rnd 3: *Sc1, 2sc in next*, repeat from * to * around. (18)
Rnd 4: *Sc2, 2sc in next*, repeat from * to * around. (24)
Rnd 5: *Sc3, 2sc in next*, repeat from * to * around. (30)
Rnd 6: *Sc4, 2sc in next*, repeat from * to * around. (36)
Rnd 7: *Sc5, 2sc in next*, repeat from * to * around. (42)
Rnd 8–Rnd 17: Sc1 in each stitch around. (42)
Rnd 18: Sc6, *sc2tog, sc4*, repeat from * to * 5 more times. (36)
Rnd 19: Sc6, *sc2tog, sc3*, repeat from * to * 5 more times. (30)
Rnd 20: Sc6, *sc2tog, sc2*, repeat from * to * 5 more times. (24)
Cut yarn of first ear. When finished with the second ear, don't cut the yarn—continue with the head instructions. Fold first ear flat after the next 3 stitches (in the center of the 6 stitches that haven't been decreased).

HEAD

Rnd 1: In second ear sc3, take the first ear and continue in the stitch after the point you folded it, sc24, continue in second ear, sc21. (48)
Rnd 2: *Sc7, 2sc in next*, repeat from * to * around. (54)
Rnd 3–Rnd 7: Sc1 in each stitch around. (54)
Rnd 8: *Sc7, sc2tog*, repeat from * to * around. (48)
Rnd 9: Sc1 in each stitch around. (48)
Rnd 10: *Sc6, sc2tog*, repeat from * to * around. (42)
Rnd 11: Sc1 in each stitch around. (42)
Rnd 12: *Sc5, sc2tog*, repeat from * to * around. (36)
Rnd 13: Sc1 in each stitch around. (36)
Rnd 14: *Sc4, sc2tog*, repeat from * to * around. (30)
Rnd 15: Sc1 in each stitch around. (30)
Rnd 16: *Sc3, sc2tog*, repeat from * to * around. (24)

Rnd 17: Sc1 in each stitch around. (24)
Rnd 18: *Sc2, sc2tog*, repeat from * to * around. (18)
Attach the safety eyes to the head between Rnd 13 and Rnd 14. Now take a piece of the blue yarn and sew across Rnd 20 of the ears to close them off so they won't be stuffed. Stuff the head.
Rnd 19–32: Sc1 in each stitch around. (18)
Stuff the trunk lightly to keep it flexible.
Rnd 33: In back loops only, *sc1, sc2tog*, repeat from * to * around. (12)
Cut the yarn, weave through the 12 remaining stitches, pull tight, and weave in ends.

BODY

Rnd 1: Ch18, 1dc in third ch from hook, dc14, 3dc in last, continue along other side of chains, dc15, 3dc in last, sl st in first dc. (36)
Rnd 2: Ch2 (doesn't count as first stitch now and throughout), *dc17, 2dc in next*, repeat from * to * one more time, sl st in first dc. (38)

Rnd 3: Ch2, *dc18, 2dc in next*, repeat from * to * one more time, sl st in first dc. (40)
Rnd 4: Ch2, *dc19, 2dc in next*, repeat from * to * one more time, sl st in first dc. (42)
Rnd 5: Ch2, *dc20, 2dc in next*, repeat from * to * one more time, sl st in first dc. (44)
Rnd 6: Ch2, *dc21, 2dc in next*, repeat from * to * one more time, sl st in first dc. (46)
Rnd 7: Ch2, *dc22, 2dc in next*, repeat from * to * one more time, sl st in first dc. (48)
Rnd 8: Ch2, *dc23, 2dc in next*, repeat from * to * one more time, sl st in first dc. (50)
Rnd 9: Ch2, *dc24, 2dc in next*, repeat from * to * one more time, sl st in first dc. (52)
Rnd 10: Ch2, *dc25, 2dc in next*, repeat from * to * one more time, sl st in first dc. (54)
Rnd 11: Ch2, *dc26, 2dc in next*, repeat from * to * one more time, sl st in first dc. (56)
Rnd 12: Ch2, *dc27, 2dc in next*, repeat from * to * one more time, sl st in first dc. (58)
Rnd 13: Ch2, *dc28, 2dc in next*, repeat from * to * one more time, sl st in first dc. (60)
Rnd 14: Ch2, *dc29, 2dc in next*, repeat from * to * one more time, sl st in first dc. (62)
Rnd 15: Ch2, *dc30, 2dc in next*, repeat from * to * one more time, sl st in first dc. (64)
Rnd 16: Ch2, *dc31, 2dc in next*, repeat from * to * one more time, sl st in first dc. (66)
Rnd 17: Ch2, *dc32, 2dc in next*, repeat from * to * one more time, sl st in first dc. (68)
Rnd 18: Ch2, *dc33, 2dc in next*, repeat from * to * one more time, sl st in first dc. (70)
Rnd 19: Ch2, *dc34, 2dc in next*, repeat from * to * one more time, sl st in first dc. (72)
Cut a long tail to close the body in the end; fold the body in line with the increases to make the belly straight.

ARMS (MAKE 2)

Rnd 1: Start with a magic ring, 6sc in the ring. (6)
Rnd 2: 2sc in each stitch around. (12)
Rnd 3: *Sc1, 2sc in next*, repeat from * to * around. (18)
Rnd 4: *Sc2, 2sc in next*, repeat from * to * around. (24)
Rnd 5–Rnd 9: Sc1 in each stitch around. (24)
Rnd 10: *Sc2, sc2tog*, repeat from * to * around. (18)
Rnd 11–Rnd 12: Sc1 in each stitch around. (18)
Rnd 13: Sl st 1, ch2 (doesn't count as first stitch now and throughout), dc1 in each stitch around, sl st in first dc. (18)
Rnd 14: Ch2, dc2tog, dc1 in each stitch around, sl st in first dc. (17)
At this point, stuff the hand and use a small piece of the blue yarn to sew across the arm between Rnd 12 and Rnd 13.
Rnd 15: Ch2, dc1 in each stitch around, sl st in first dc. (17)
Rnd 16: Ch2, dc2tog, dc1 in each stitch around, sl st in first dc. (16)
Rnd 17: Ch2, dc1 in each stitch around, sl st in first dc. (16)
Rnd 18: Ch2, dc2tog, dc1 in each stitch around, sl st in first dc. (15)
Rnd 19: Ch2, dc1 in each stitch around, sl st in first dc. (15)
Rnd 20: Ch2, dc2tog, dc1 in each stitch around, sl st in first dc. (14)
Rnd 21: Ch2, dc1 in each stitch around, sl st in first dc. (14)
Rnd 22: Ch2, dc2tog, dc1 in each stitch around, sl st in first dc. (13)
Cut a long tail to attach the arms to the body later.

LEGS (MAKE 2)

Rnd 1: Start with a magic ring, ch2, 12dc in the ring, sl st in first dc. (12)
Rnd 2: Ch2, *dc1, 2dc in next*, repeat from * to * around, sl st in first dc. (18)
Rnd 3–Rnd 7: Ch2, dc1 in each stitch around, sl st in first dc. (18)
Cut yarn and weave in ends.

PUTTING IT ALL TOGETHER

- Place both legs between the bottom two layers of the body, and then use the remaining yarn from the body to sew across the seam, with the legs in between, to close the body and at the same time attach the legs.
- Sew an arm to each side of the body between Rnd 1 and Rnd 3.
- Sew Rnd 14 of the head (ears not included) to Rnd 1 of the body.

HORSE

Trot, trot, trot. I love to gallop and run!

DIMENSIONS

14.6 in. (37 cm) long and 6.7 in. (17 cm) wide

MATERIALS

DK #3 lightweight yarn (sample shown in Scheepjes Stone Washed):
- beige (Boulder Opal): 164 yd. (150 m)
- white (Moon Stone): 109.4 yd. (100 m)
- black (Black Onyx): 54.7 yd. (50 m)

Crochet hook: US size D-3 (3 mm)
Brown and black safety eyes, 15 mm
Black safety eyes, 10 mm (for nostrils)
Fiberfill stuffing
Yarn needle and scissors

DIFFICULTY LEVEL

FIRST EAR

Rnd 1: With beige, start with a magic ring, 6sc in the ring. (6)
Rnd 2: Sc1 in each stitch around. (6)
Rnd 3: 2sc in each stitch around. (12)
Rnd 4–Rnd 5: Sc1 in each stitch around. (12)
Rnd 6: *Sc1, 2sc in next*, repeat from * to * around. (18)
Rnd 7: Sc1 in each stitch around. (18)
Cut the thread and weave in the ends.

SECOND EAR

Rnd 1: With beige, start with a magic ring, 6sc in the ring. (6)
Rnd 2: Sc1 in each stitch around. (6)
Rnd 3: 2sc in each stitch around. (12)
Rnd 4–Rnd 5: Sc1 in each stitch around. (12)
Rnd 6: *Sc1, 2sc in next*, repeat from * to * around. (18)
Rnd 7: Sc1 in each stitch around. (18)
Do not cut the yarn!

HEAD

Crochet with the **beige** yarn of the second ear to form the top of the head.
Rnd 1: Ch9, take the first ear, sc in all 18 stitches of the first ear, sc in the other side of each of the 9 chains you just crocheted, sc in each of the 18 stitches of the second ear. (54)
Rnd 2: Sc1 in each stitch around. (54)
Rnd 3: Sc18, sc2tog, sc25, sc2tog, sc7. (52)
Rnd 4: Sc in each round stitch around. (52)
Rnd 5: Sc18, sc2tog, sc24, sc2tog, sc6. (50)
Rnd 6: Sc1 in each stitch around. (50)
Rnd 7: Sc18, sc2tog, sc23, sc2tog, sc5. (48)
Rnd 8: Sc1 in each stitch around. (48)
Rnd 9: Sc18, sc2tog, sc22, sc2tog, sc4. (46)
Rnd 10: Sc1 in each stitch around. (46)
Rnd 11: Sc18, sc2tog, sc21, sc2tog, sc3. (44)
Rnd 12: Sc1 in each stitch around. (44)

Rnd 13: Sc18, sc2tog, sc20, sc2tog, sc2. (42)
Rnd 14: Sc1 in each stitch around. (42)
Rnd 15: Sc18, sc2tog, sc19, sc2tog, sc1. (40)
Rnd 16: Sc1 in each stitch around. (40)
Rnd 17: Sc18, sc2tog, sc18, sc2tog. (38)
Rnd 18: Sc1 in each stitch around. (38)
Rnd 19: Sc2tog, sc16, sc2tog, sc18. (36)
Rnd 20: Change color to **white**, sc1 in each stitch around. (36)
Rnd 21–Rnd 24: Sc1 in each stitch around. (36)
Rnd 25: *Sc4, sc2tog*, repeat from * to * around. (30)
Rnd 26: *Sc3, sc2tog*, repeat from * to * around. (24)
Rnd 27: *Sc2, sc2tog*, repeat from * to * around. (18)
Attach the brown and black safety eyes between Rnd 10 and Rnd 11 of the head; stuff the head.
Rnd 28: *Sc1, sc2tog*, repeat from * to * around. (12)
Attach the black safety eyes as nostrils between Rnd 26 and Rnd 27.
Fold the seam flat and sew the front and back of the head against each other.

BODY

Rnd 1: With beige ch18, dc1 in third ch from hook, dc14, 3dc in last, continue along other side of chains, dc15, 3dc in last, sl st in first dc. (36)
Rnd 2: Ch2 (does not count as first stitch for the entire pattern), *dc17, 2dc in next*, repeat from * to * 1 more time, sl st in first dc. (38)
Rnd 3: With beige ch2, dc3, **with white** dc12, **with beige** dc3, 2dc in next, dc18, 2dc in next, sl st in first dc. (40)
Rnd 4: With beige ch2, dc3, **with white** dc13, **with beige** dc3, 2dc in next, dc19, 2dc in next, sl st in first dc. (42)
Rnd 5: With beige ch2, dc3, **with white** dc14, **with beige** dc3, 2dc in next, dc20, 2dc in next, sl st in first dc. (44)
Rnd 6: With beige ch2, dc3, **with white** dc15, **with beige** dc3, 2dc in next, dc21, 2dc in next, sl st in first dc. (46)
Rnd 7: With beige ch2, dc3, **with white** dc16, **with beige** dc3, 2dc in next, dc22, 2dc in next, sl st in first dc. (48)
Rnd 8: With beige ch2, dc3, **with white** dc17, **with beige** dc3, 2dc in next, dc23, 2dc in next, sl st in first dc. (50)
Rnd 9: With beige ch2, dc3, **with white** dc18, **with beige** dc3, 2dc in next, dc24, 2dc in next, sl st in first dc. (52)
Rnd 10: With beige ch2, dc3, **with white** dc19, **with beige** dc3, 2dc in next, dc25, 2dc in next, sl st in first dc. (54)
Rnd 11: With beige ch2, dc3, **with white** dc20, **with beige** dc3, 2dc in next, dc26, 2dc in next, sl st in first dc. (56)
Rnd 12: With beige ch2, dc3, **with white** dc21, **with beige** dc3, 2dc in next, dc27, 2dc in next, sl st in first dc. (58)
Rnd 13: With beige ch2, dc3, **with white** dc22, **with beige** dc3, 2dc in next, dc28, 2dc in next, sl st in first dc. (60)
Rnd 14: With beige ch2, dc3, **with white** dc23, **with beige** dc3, 2dc in next, dc29, 2dc in next, sl st in first dc. (62)
Rnd 15: With beige ch2, dc3, **with white** dc24, **with beige** dc3, 2dc in next, dc30, 2dc in next, sl st in first dc. (64)
Rnd 16: With beige ch2, dc3, **with white** dc25, **with beige** dc3, 2dc in next, dc31, 2dc in next, sl st in first dc. (66)
Rnd 17: With beige ch2, dc3, **with white** dc26, **with beige** dc3, 2dc in next, dc32, 2dc in next, sl st in first dc. (68)
Rnd 18: With beige ch2, dc3, **with white** dc27, **with beige** dc3, 2dc in next, dc33, 2dc in next, sl st in first dc. (70)
Rnd 19: With beige ch2, dc3, **with white** dc28, **with beige** dc3, 2dc in next, dc34, 2dc in next, sl st in first dc. (72)
Rnd 20: With beige ch2, *dc35, 2dc in next*, repeat from * to * 1 more time, sl st in first dc. (74)
Cut a long piece of yarn to close the body at the end and fold it in half on the line of increases.

ARMS (MAKE 2)

Rnd 1: With black, start with a magic ring, 6sc in the ring. (6)
Rnd 2: 2sc in each stitch around. (12)
Rnd 3: *Sc1, 2sc in next*, repeat from * to * around. (18)
Rnd 4: *Sc2, 2sc in next*, repeat from * to * around. (24)
Rnd 5: Working in back loops only, sc1 in every stitch around. (24)
Rnd 6–Rnd 9: Sc1 in each stitch around. (24)
Rnd 10: *Sc2, sc2tog*, repeat from * to * around. (18)
Rnd 11: Sc1 in each stitch around. (18)
Cut a long yarn to use after Rnd 13.
Rnd 12: With brown sl st, ch2, dc1 in each stitch around, sl st in first dc. (18)
Rnd 13: Ch2, dc2tog, dc1 in each stitch around, sl st in first dc. (17)
Fill up the hand and sew the arm shut between Rnd 11 and Rnd 12.
Rnd 14: Ch2, dc1 in each stitch around, sl st in first dc. (17)
Rnd 15: Ch2, dc2tog, dc1 in each stitch around, sl st in first dc. (16)
Rnd 16: Ch2, dc1 in each stitch around, sl st in first dc. (16)
Rnd 17: Ch2, dc2tog, dc1 in each stitch around, sl st in first dc. (15)
Rnd 18: Ch2, dc1 in each stitch around, sl st in first dc. (15)
Rnd 19: Ch2, dc2tog, dc1 in every stitch around, sl st in first dc. (14)
Rnd 20: Ch2, dc1 in each stitch around, sl st in first dc. (14)
Rnd 21: Ch2, dc2tog, dc1 in every stitch around, sl st in first dc. (13)
Cut a long tail to attach the arms later.

LEGS (MAKE 2)

Rnd 1: With black, start with a magic ring, 6sc in the ring. (6)
Rnd 2: 2sc in each stitch around. (12)
Rnd 3: *Sc1, 2sc in next*, repeat from * to * around. (18)
Rnd 4: *Sc2, 2sc in next*, repeat from * to * around. (24)
Rnd 5: Working in back loops only, sc1 in each stitch around. (24)
Rnd 6–Rnd 9: Sc1 in each stitch around. (24)
Rnd 10: *Sc2, sc2tog*, repeat from * to * around. (18)
Rnd 11: Sc1 in each stitch around. (18)
Cut a long tail to use after Rnd 13.
Rnd 12: With brown sl st, ch2, dc1 in each stitch around, sl st in first dc. (18)
Rnd 13: Ch2, dc2tog, dc1 in each stitch around, sl st in first dc. (17)
Fill up the foot and sew the leg tightly between Rnd 11 and Rnd 12.
Rnd 14: Ch2, dc1 in each stitch around, sl st in first dc. (17)
Rnd 15: Ch2, dc2tog, dc1 in each stitch around, sl st in first dc. (16)
Rnd 16: Ch2, dc1 in each stitch around, sl st in first dc. (16)
Rnd 17: Ch2, dc2tog, dc1 in each stitch around, sl st in first dc. (15)
Cut the yarn and weave in the ends.

PUTTING IT ALL TOGETHER

- Place the legs between the two layers at the bottom of the body and close the seam with the legs in between.
- Sew an arm on each side of the body between Rnd 2 and Rnd 4.
- Attach the mane by cutting pieces of white yarn of approximately 10 in. (25 cm), hold it double, insert the hook into the stitch, pull the yarn through the hole at the center, hold it on the hook, and thread the ends through the loop on the hook to make a knot. Now repeat this over the head in the part between the ears, from Rnd 2 on the forehead to Rnd 10 on the back of the head in rows of 7 to 8 stitches.
- Sew Rnd 16 of the head (ears not counted) against Rnd 1 of the body.

MOUSE

Cupcake and tea?

DIMENSIONS

13.8 in. (35 cm) high (including ears) and 6.7 in. (17 cm) wide

MATERIALS

DK #3 lightweight yarn (sample shown in Scheepjes Stone Washed):
- brown (Boulder Opal): 251.5 yd. (230 m)
- white (Moon Stone): 142.2 yd. (130 m)

Crochet hook: US size D-3 (3 mm)
Black and blue safety eyes, 15 mm
Pink safety nose, 15 mm wide
Fiberfill stuffing
Yarn needle and scissors

DIFFICULTY LEVEL

EARS (MAKE 2)

Rnd 1: With brown, start with a magic ring, 6sc in the ring. (6)
Rnd 2: 2sc in each stitch around. (12)
Rnd 3: *Sc1, 2sc in next*, repeat from * to * around. (18)
Rnd 4: *Sc2, 2sc in next*, repeat from * to * around. (24)
Rnd 5: *Sc3, 2sc in next*, repeat from * to * around. (30)
Rnd 6: *Sc4, 2sc in next*, repeat from * to * around. (36)
Rnd 7: *Sc5, 2sc in next*, repeat from * to * around. (42)
Rnd 8–Rnd 17: Sc1 in each stitch around. (42)
Rnd 18: Sc6, *sc2tog, sc4*, repeat from * to * 5 more times. (36)
Rnd 19: Sc6, *sc2tog, sc3*, repeat from * to * 5 more times. (30)
Rnd 20: Sc6, *sc2tog, sc2*, repeat from * to * 5 more times. (24)
Cut yarn of the first ear. When finished with the second ear, don't cut the yarn—continue with the head instructions. Fold the first ear flat after the next 3 stitches (in the center of the 6 stitches that haven't been decreased).

HEAD

Rnd 1: In second ear sc3, take the first ear and continue in the stitch after the point you folded it, sc24, continue in second ear, sc21. (48)
Rnd 2: *Sc7, 2sc in next*, repeat from * to * around. (54)
Rnd 3: Sc1 in each stitch around. (54)
Rnd 4: *Sc16, sc2tog*, repeat from * to * 2 more times. (51)
Rnd 5: Sc1 in each stitch around. (51)
Rnd 6: *Sc15, sc2tog*, repeat from * to * 2 more times. (48)
Rnd 7: Sc1 in each stitch around. (48)
Rnd 8: *Sc14, sc2tog*, repeat from * to * 2 more times. (45)

Rnd 9: Sc1 in each stitch around. (45)
Rnd 10: *Sc13, sc2tog*, repeat from * to * 2 more times. (42)
Rnd 11: Sc1 in each stitch around. (42)
Rnd 12: *Sc12, sc2tog*, repeat from * to * 2 more times. (39)
Rnd 13: Sc1 in each stitch around. (39)
Rnd 14: *Sc11, sc2tog*, repeat from * to * 2 more times. (36)
Rnd 15: Sc1 in each stitch around. (36)
Rnd 16: *Sc10, sc2tog*, repeat from * to * 2 more times. (33)
Rnd 17: Sc1 in each stitch around. (33)
Rnd 18: *Sc9, sc2tog*, repeat from * to * 2 more times. (30)
Rnd 19: Sc1 in each stitch around. (30)
Rnd 20: *Sc8, sc2tog*, repeat from * to * 2 more times. (27)

Rnd 21: Sc1 in each stitch around. (27)
Rnd 22: *Sc7, sc2tog*, repeat from * to * 2 more times. (24)
Rnd 23: Sc1 in each stitch around. (24)
Rnd 24: *Sc6, sc2tog*, repeat from * to * 2 more times. (21)
Rnd 25: Sc1 in each stitch around. (21)
Rnd 26: *Sc5, sc2tog*, repeat from * to * 2 more times. (18)
Rnd 27: Sc1 in each stitch around. (18)
Attach the safety eyes to the head between Rnd 6 and Rnd 7. Now take a piece of brown yarn and sew across the top of the head to close off the ears so they won't be stuffed. Stuff the head.
Rnd 28: *Sc1, sc2tog*, repeat from * to * around. (12)
Attach the safety nose between Rnd 27 and Rnd 28. Cut the yarn, weave through the 12 remaining stitches, pull tight, and weave in ends.

BODY

Rnd 1: With brown ch18, 1dc in third ch from hook, dc14, 3dc in last, continue along other side of chains, dc15, 3dc in last, sl st in first dc. (36)
Rnd 2: Ch2 (doesn't count as first stitch now and throughout), dc3, **with white** dc11, **with brown** dc3, 2dc in next, dc17, 2dc in next, sl st in first dc. (38)
Rnd 3: With brown ch2, dc3, **with white** dc12, **with brown** dc3, 2dc in next, dc18, 2dc in next, sl st in first dc. (40)
Rnd 4: With brown ch2, dc3, **with white** dc13, **with brown** dc3, 2dc in next, dc19, 2dc in next, sl st in first dc. (42)
Rnd 5: With brown ch2, dc3, **with white** dc14, **with brown** dc3, 2dc in next, dc20, 2dc in next, sl st in first dc. (44)
Rnd 6: With brown ch2, dc3, **with white** dc15, **with brown** dc3, 2dc in next, dc21, 2dc in next, sl st in first dc. (46)
Rnd 7: With brown ch2, dc3, **with white** dc16, **with brown** dc3, 2dc in next, dc22, 2dc in next, sl st in first dc. (48)
Rnd 8: With brown ch2, dc3, **with white** dc17, **with brown** dc3, 2dc in next, dc23, 2dc in next, sl st in first dc. (50)
Rnd 9: With brown ch2, dc3, **with white** dc18, **with brown** dc3, 2dc in next, dc24, 2dc in next, sl st in first dc. (52)
Rnd 10: With brown ch2, dc3, **with white** dc19, **with brown** dc3, 2dc in next, dc25, 2dc in next, sl st in first dc. (54)
Rnd 11: With brown ch2, dc3, **with white** dc20, **with brown** dc3, 2dc in next, dc26, 2dc in next, sl st in first dc. (56)

Rnd 12: With brown ch2, dc3, **with white** dc21, **with brown** dc3, 2dc in next, dc27, 2dc in next, sl st in first dc. (58)
Rnd 13: With brown ch2, dc3, **with white** dc22, **with brown** dc3, 2dc in next, dc28, 2dc in next, sl st in first dc. (60)
Rnd 14: With brown ch2, dc3, **with white** dc23, **with brown** dc3, 2dc in next, dc29, 2dc in next, sl st in first dc. (62)
Rnd 15: With brown ch2, dc3, **with white** dc24, **with brown** dc3, 2dc in next, dc30, 2dc in next, sl st in first dc. (64)
Rnd 16: With brown ch2, dc3, **with white** dc25, **with brown** dc3, 2dc in next, dc31, 2dc in next, sl st in first dc. (66)
Rnd 17: With brown ch2, dc3, **with white** dc26, **with brown** dc3, 2dc in next, dc32, 2dc in next, sl st in first dc. (68)
Rnd 18: With brown ch2, dc3, **with white** dc27, **with brown** dc3, 2dc in next, dc33, 2dc in next, sl st in first dc. (70)
Rnd 19: With brown ch2, *dc34, 2dc in next*, repeat from * to * around, sl st in first dc. (72)
Cut a long tail to close the body in the end; fold the body in line with the increases to make the belly straight.

ARMS (MAKE 2)

Rnd 1: With white, start with a magic ring, 6sc in the ring. (6)
Rnd 2: 2sc in each stitch around. (12)
Rnd 3: *Sc1, 2sc in next*, repeat from * to * around. (18)
Rnd 4: *Sc2, 2sc in next*, repeat from * to * around. (24)
Rnd 5–Rnd 9: Sc1 in each stitch around. (24)
Rnd 10: *Sc2, sc2tog*, repeat from * to * around. (18)
Rnd 11–Rnd 12: Sc1 in each stitch around. (18)
Cut a long tail of the white yarn; you'll need it after Rnd 14.
Rnd 13: With brown sl st 1, ch2 (doesn't count as first stitch now and throughout), dc1 in each stitch around, sl st in first dc. (18)
Rnd 14: Ch2, dc2tog, dc1 in each stitch around, sl st in first dc. (17)
At this point, stuff the hand and use the yarn from Rnd 12 to sew across the arm between Rnd 12 and Rnd 13.
Rnd 15: Ch2, dc1 in each stitch around, sl st in first dc. (17)
Rnd 16: Ch2, dc2tog, dc1 in each stitch around, sl st in first dc. (16)
Rnd 17: Ch2, dc1 in each stitch around, sl st in first dc. (16)
Rnd 18: Ch2, dc2tog, dc1 in each stitch around, sl st in first dc. (15)
Rnd 19: Ch2, dc1 in each stitch around, sl st in first dc. (15)
Rnd 20: Ch2, dc2tog, dc1 in each stitch around, sl st in first dc. (14)
Rnd 21: Ch2, dc1 in each stitch around, sl st in first dc. (14)
Rnd 22: Ch2, dc2tog, dc1 in each stitch around, sl st in first dc. (13)
Cut a long tail to attach arms to body later.

LEGS (MAKE 2)

Rnd 1: With white, start with a magic ring, ch2, 12dc in the loop, sl st in first dc. (12)
Rnd 2: Ch2, *dc1, 2dc in next*, repeat from * to * around, sl st in first dc. (18)
Rnd 3: Ch2, dc1 in each stitch around, sl st in first dc. (18)
Rnd 4–Rnd 7: With brown ch2, dc1 in each stitch around, sl st in first dc. (18)
Cut yarn and weave in ends.

PUTTING IT ALL TOGETHER

- Place both legs between the bottom two layers of the body and use the remaining yarn from the body to sew across the seam, with legs in between, to close the body and at the same time attach the legs.
- Sew an arm to each side of the body between Rnd 2 and Rnd 4.
- Sew Rnd 10 of the head to Rnd 1 of the body.

Get to know this panda, and she'll be your friend for life.

DIMENSIONS

13 in. 33 (cm) long and 6.3 in. (16 cm) wide

MATERIALS

DK #3 lightweight yarn (sample shown in Scheepjes Stone Washed):
- black (Black Onyx): 142.2 yd. (130 m)
- white (Moon Stone): 142.2 yd. (130 m)

Crochet hook: US size D-3 (3 mm)
Black and blue safety eyes, 12 mm
Black safety nose, 15 mm wide
Fiberfill stuffing
Yarn needle and scissors

DIFFICULTY LEVEL

EYES (MAKE 2)

Rnd 1: With black, start with a magic ring, 6sc in the ring. (6) *Don't pull the ring too tight; you'll put the safety eyes through the center later.*

Rnd 2: 2sc in each stitch around. (12)
Rnd 3: *Sc1, 2sc in next*, repeat from * to * around. (18)
Rnd 4: *Sc2, 2sc in next*, repeat from * to * around. (24)
Put the safety eyes though the center of Rnd 1. Don't attach the closure yet; continue with the head.

HEAD

Rnd 1: With white, start with a magic ring, 6sc in the ring. (6)
Rnd 2: 2sc in each stitch around. (12)
Rnd 3: *Sc1, 2sc in next*, repeat from * to * around. (18)
Rnd 4: *Sc2, 2sc in next*, repeat from * to * around. (24)
Rnd 5: *Sc3, 2sc in next*, repeat from * to * around. (30)
Rnd 6: *Sc4, 2sc in next*, repeat from * to * around. (36)
Rnd 7: *Sc5, 2sc in next*, repeat from * to * around. (42)
Rnd 8: *Sc6, 2sc in next*, repeat from * to * around. (48)
Rnd 9: *Sc7, 2sc in next*, repeat from * to * around. (54)
Rnd 10: *Sc8, 2sc in next*, repeat from * to * around. (60)
Rnd 11–Rnd 20: Sc1 in each stitch around. (60)
Rnd 21: *Sc8, sc2tog*, repeat from * to * around. (54)
Rnd 22: *Sc7, sc2tog*, repeat from * to * around. (48)
Rnd 23: *Sc6, sc2tog*, repeat from * to * around. (42)
Rnd 24: *Sc5, sc2tog*, repeat from * to * around. (36)
Rnd 25: *Sc4, sc2tog*, repeat from * to * around. (30)
Rnd 26: *Sc3, sc2tog*, repeat from * to * around. (24)
Rnd 27: *Sc2, sc2tog*, repeat from * to * around. (18)
Put the safety eyes through the head between Rnd 18 and Rnd 19, and attach the closures inside the head. Stuff the head, but not too firm, so you can press it flat and mold it in shape.
Rnd 28: *Sc1, sc2tog*, repeat from * to * around. (12)
Cut a long tail and sew the seam closed. Sew along the edge of the eyes with the remaining yarn.

NOSE

Rnd 1: With white, start with a magic ring, 6sc in the ring. (6)
Rnd 2: 2sc in each stitch around. (12)
Rnd 3: *Sc1, 2sc in next*, repeat from * to * around. (18)
Rnd 4: *Sc2, 2sc in next*, repeat from * to * around. (24)
Rnd 5: Sc1 in each stitch around. (24)
Cut a long tail, attach the safety nose in Rnd 3, stuff the nose, and sew the nose to the head.

EARS (MAKE 2)

Rnd 1: With black, start with a magic ring, 6sc in the ring. (6)
Rnd 2: 2sc in each stitch around. (12)
Rnd 3: *Sc1, 2sc in next*, repeat from * to * around. (18)
Rnd 4: *Sc2, 2sc in next*, repeat from * to * around. (24)
Rnd 5–Rnd 9: Sc1 in each stitch around. (24)
Cut a long tail, stuff the ears lightly, and sew an ear to each side of the head between Rnd 6 and Rnd 14.

BODY

Rnd 1: With black ch18, 1dc in third ch from hook, dc14, 3dc in last, continue along other side of chains, dc15, 3dc in last, sl st in first dc. (36)
Rnd 2: Ch2 (doesn't count as first stitch for entire pattern), *dc17, 2dc in next*, repeat from * to * one more time, sl st in first dc. (38)
Rnd 3: Ch2, *dc18, 2dc in next*, repeat from * to * one more time, sl st in first dc. (40)
Rnd 4: Ch2, *dc19, 2dc in next*, repeat from * to * one more time, sl st in first dc. (42)
Rnd 5: Ch2, *dc20, 2dc in next*, repeat from * to * one more time, sl st in first dc. (44) Cut the black yarn.
Rnd 6: With white ch2, *dc21, 2dc in next*, repeat from * to * one more time, sl st in first dc. (46)
Rnd 7: Ch2, *dc22, 2dc in next*, repeat from * to * one more time, sl st in first dc. (48)
Rnd 8: Ch2, *dc23, 2dc in next*, repeat from * to * one more time, sl st in first dc. (50)
Rnd 9: Ch2, *dc24, 2dc in next*, repeat from * to * one more time, sl st in first dc. (52)
Rnd 10: Ch2, *dc25, 2dc in next*, repeat from * to * one more time, sl st in first dc. (54)
Rnd 11: Ch2, *dc26, 2dc in next*, repeat from * to * one more time, sl st in first dc. (56)
Rnd 12: Ch2, *dc27, 2dc in next*, repeat from * to * one more time, sl st in first dc. (58)
Rnd 13: Ch2, *dc28, 2dc in next*, repeat from * to * one more time, sl st in first dc. (60)
Rnd 14: Ch2, *dc29, 2dc in next*, repeat from * to * one more time, sl st in first dc. (62)
Rnd 15: Ch2, *dc30, 2dc in next*, repeat from * to * one more time, sl st in first dc. (64)
Rnd 16: Ch2, *dc31, 2dc in next*, repeat from * to * one more time, sl st in first dc. (66)
Rnd 17: Ch2, *dc32, 2dc in next*, repeat from * to * one more time, sl st in first dc. (68)
Rnd 18: Ch2, *dc33, 2dc in next*, repeat from * to * one more time, sl st in first dc. (70)
Rnd 19: Ch2, *dc34, 2dc in next*, repeat from * to * one more time, sl st in first dc. (72)
Rnd 20: Ch2, *dc35, 2dc in next*, repeat from * to * one more time, sl st in first dc. (74)
Cut a long tail to close the body in the end.

ARMS (MAKE 2)

Rnd 1: With black, start with a magic ring, 6sc in the ring. (6)
Rnd 2: 2sc in each stitch around. (12)
Rnd 3: *Sc1, 2sc in next*, repeat from * to * around. (18)
Rnd 4: *Sc2, 2sc in next*, repeat from * to * around. (24)
Rnd 5–Rnd 9: Sc1 in each stitch around. (24)
Rnd 10: *Sc2, sc2tog*, repeat from * to * around. (18)
Rnd 11–Rnd 12: Sc1 in each stitch around. (18)
Rnd 13: Sl st 1, ch2 (doesn't count as first stitch now and thourghout), dc1 in each stitch around, sl st in first dc. (18)
Rnd 14: Ch2, dc2tog, dc1 in each stitch around, sl st in first dc. (17)
At this point, stuff the hand (not too much) and use a small piece of yarn to sew across the arm between Rnd 12 and Rnd 13.
Rnd 15: Ch2, dc1 in each stitch around, sl st in first dc. (17)
Rnd 16: Ch2, dc2tog, dc1 in each stitch around, sl st in first dc. (16)
Rnd 17: Ch2, dc1 in each stitch around, sl st in first dc. (16)
Rnd 18: Ch2, dc2tog, dc1 in each stitch around, sl st in first dc. (15)
Rnd 19: Ch2, dc1 in each stitch around, sl st in first dc. (15)
Rnd 20: Ch2, dc2tog, dc1 in each stitch around, sl st in first dc. (14)
Rnd 21: Ch2, dc1 in each stitch around, sl st in first dc. (14)
Rnd 22: Ch2, dc2tog, dc1 in each stitch around, sl st in first dc. (13)
Cut a long tail to attach arms to body in the end.

LEGS (MAKE 2)

Rnd 1: With black, start with a magic ring, ch2, 12dc in the ring, sl st in first dc. (12)
Rnd 2: Ch2, *dc1, 2dc in next*, repeat from * to * around, sl st in first dc. (18)
Rnd 3–Rnd 7: Ch2, dc1 in each stitch around, sl st in first dc. (18)
Cut yarn and weave in ends.

PUTTING IT ALL TOGETHER

- Place both legs between the bottom two layers of the body and use the remaining yarn from the body to sew across the seam, with the legs in between, to close the body and at the same time attach legs.
- Sew an arm to each side of the body between Rnd 1 and Rnd 4.
- Sew Rnd 23 of the head to Rnd 1 of the body.

PRINCESS

Every princess needs a friend.

DIMENSIONS

15 in. (38 cm) long and 5.9 in. (15 cm) wide

MATERIALS

DK #3 lightweight yarn (sample shown in Scheepjes Stone Washed):

- hair color (Yellow Jasper): 109.4 yd. (100 m)
- pink (Corondum Ruby): 164 yd. (150 m)
- red (Red Jasper): 54.7 yd. (50 m)
- skin color (Softfun 2466): 87.5 yd. (80 m)

Crochet hook: US size D-3 (3 mm)
Black and blue safety eyes, 12 mm
Small amount of fiberfill stuffing
Yarn needle and scissors

DIFFICULTY LEVEL

HAIR AND HEAD

Rnd 1: With hair color, start with a magic ring, 6sc in the ring. (6)
Rnd 2: 2sc in each stitch around. (12)
Rnd 3: *Sc1, 2sc in next*, repeat from * to * around. (18)
Rnd 4: *Sc2, 2sc in next*, repeat from * to * around. (24)
Rnd 5–Rnd 8: Sc1 in each stitch around. (24)
Rnd 9: *Ch6, sc in second ch from hook, sc4, continue in Rnd 8, sc12*, repeat from * to * one more time. (34)
You will now continue in both sides of the chains and the bun to form the top of the head.
Rnd 10: ***In first side of chains**, sc5; **in other side of chains**, 4sc in next, sc4; **in bun**, sc12*, repeat from * to * one more time. (50)
Rnd 11–Rnd 15: Sc1 in each stitch around. (50)
Rnd 16: Sc17, **with skin color** sc1, **with hair color** sc32. (50)
Rnd 17: Sc17, **with skin color** sc3, **with hair color** sc30. (50)
Rnd 18: Sc17, **with skin color** sc5, **with hair color** sc28. (50)
Rnd 19: Sc16, **with skin color** sc8, **with hair color** sc26. (50)
Rnd 20: Sc15, **with skin color** sc11, **with hair color** sc24. (50)
Rnd 21: Sc14, **with skin color** sc14, **with hair color** sc22. (50)
Rnd 22: Sc13, **with skin color** sc17, **with hair color** sc20. (50)
Rnd 23: Sc12, **with skin color** sc20, **with hair color** sc18. (50)
Rnd 24: Sc11, **with skin color** sc23, **with hair color** sc16. (50)
Rnd 25: Sc10, **with skin color** sc40. (50)
Cut the hair color yarn.
Rnd 26: *Sc6, sc2tog*, repeat from * to * to last 2 stitches, sc2. (44)
Rnd 27: *Sc5, sc2tog*, repeat from * to * to last 2 stitches, sc2. (38)
Rnd 28: *Sc4, sc2tog*, repeat from * to * to last 2 stitches, sc2. (32)
Rnd 29: *Sc3, sc2tog*, repeat from * to * to last 2 stitches, sc2. (26)
Rnd 30: *Sc2, sc2tog*, repeat from * to * to last 2 stitches, sc2. (20)
Attach eyes between Rnd 22 and Rnd 23 with 10 stitches between them and stuff the head.
Rnd 31: *Sc1, sc2tog*, repeat from * to * to last 2 stitches, sc2. (14)
Cut a long tail, fold the opening horizontally, and sew the seam closed.

BODY

Rnd 1: With pink ch18, dc in 3rd ch from hook, dc14, 3dc in last, continue along other side of chains, dc15, 3dc in last, sl st in first dc. (36)
Rnd 2: Ch2 (doesn't count as first stitch for entire pattern), *dc17, 2dc in next*, repeat from * to * one more time, sl st in first dc. (38)
Rnd 3: Ch2, *dc18, 2dc in next*, repeat from * to * one more time, sl st in first dc. (40)
Rnd 4: Ch2, *dc19, 2dc in next*, repeat from * to * one more time, sl st in first dc. (42)
Rnd 5: With red ch2, dc9, bow (*ch3, 3dc in same st as ch3, ch2, sl st in same st as 3dc*, rep from * to *), dc11, 2dc in next, dc20, 2dc in next, sl st in first dc. (44)
Cut the red yarn.
Rnd 6: With pink ch2, dc9, **now dc1 around the center of the bow into the stitch below**, dc11, 2dc in next, dc21, 2dc in next, sl st in first dc. (46)
Rnd 7: Ch2, *dc22, 2dc in next*, repeat from * to * one more time, sl st in first dc. (48)
Rnd 8: Ch2, *dc23, 2dc in next*, repeat from * to * one more time, sl st in first dc. (50)
Rnd 9: Ch2, *dc24, 2dc in next*, repeat from * to * one more time, sl st in first dc. (52)
Rnd 10: Ch2, *dc25, 2dc in next*, repeat from * to * one more time, sl st in first dc. (54)
Rnd 11: Ch2, *dc26, 2dc in next*, repeat from * to * one more time, sl st in first dc. (56)
Rnd 12: Ch2, *dc27, 2dc in next*, repeat from * to * one more time, sl st in first dc. (58)
Rnd 13: Ch2, *dc28, 2dc in next*, repeat from * to * one more time, sl st in first dc. (60)
Rnd 14: Ch2, *dc29, 2dc in next*, repeat from * to * one more time, sl st in first dc. (62)
Rnd 15: Ch2, *dc30, 2dc in next*, repeat from * to * one more time, sl st in first dc. (64)
Rnd 16: Ch2, *dc31, 2dc in next*, repeat from * to * one more time, sl st in first dc. (66)
Rnd 17: Ch2, *dc32, 2dc in next*, repeat from * to * one more time, sl st in first dc. (68)
Rnd 18: Ch2, *dc33, 2dc in next*, repeat from * to * one more time, sl st in first dc. (70)
Rnd 19: Ch2, *dc34, 2dc in next*, repeat from * to * one more time, sl st in first dc. (72)
Rnd 20: In front loops only, ch1, *skip 2, 7dc in next, skip 2, sc1*, repeat from * to * around, sl st in first ch. (12 scallops)
Rnd 21: Attach red yarn in unworked back loops of Rnd 19, ch2, *dc35, 2dc in next*, repeat from * to * one more time, sl st in first dc. (74)
Cut the pink yarn.
Rnd 22: Ch2, *dc36, 2dc in next*, repeat from * to * one more time, sl st in first dc. (76)
Cut a long tail to close the body and attach the feet in the end.

FEET (MAKE 2)

Rnd 1: With red, start with a magic ring, 6sc in the ring. (6)
Rnd 2: 2sc in each stitch around. (12)
Rnd 3: *Sc1, 2sc in next*, repeat from * to * around. (18)
Rnd 4: With skin color sc3, **with red** sc15. (18)
Rnd 5: With skin color sc4, **with red** sc14. (18)
Rnd 6: With skin color sc5, **with red** sc13. (18)
Rnd 7–Rnd 8: With skin color sc1 in each stitch around. (18)
Cut yarn, weave in ends, and stuff feet lightly.

ARMS (MAKE 2)

Rnd 1: With skin color, start with a magic ring, 6sc in the ring. (6)
Rnd 2: 2sc in each stitch around. (12)
Rnd 3: *Sc1, 2sc in next*, repeat from * to * around. (18)
Rnd 4–Rnd 10: Sc1 in each stitch around. (18)
Cut a long tail to use after Rnd 12.
Rnd 11: With pink sl st 1, ch2, dc1 in each stitch around, sl st in first dc. (18)
Rnd 12: Ch2, dc2tog, dc1 in each stitch around, sl st in first dc. (17)
Now stuff the hand and sew across the arm between Rnd 10 and Rnd 11.
Rnd 13: Ch2, dc1 in each stitch around, sl st in first dc. (17)
Rnd 14: Ch2, dc2tog, dc1 in each stitch around, sl st in first dc. (16)
Rnd 15: Ch2, dc1 in each stitch around, sl st in first dc. (16)
Rnd 16: Ch2, dc2tog, dc1 in each stitch around, sl st in first dc. (15)
Rnd 17: Ch2, dc1 in each stitch around, sl st in first dc. (15)
Rnd 18: Ch2, dc2tog, dc1 in each stitch around, sl st in first dc. (14)
Rnd 19: Ch2, dc1 in each stitch around, sl st in first dc. (14)
Cut a long tail to attach arms to body in the end.

CROWN

With red, ch30 (or number of chains that will fit around the bun), sl st in first ch to close the circle, sc1, hdc1, in next: (ch1, dc1, ch1, tr1, ch1, dc1, ch1), hdc1, sc1, and sew to princess's bun.

PUTTING IT ALL TOGETHER

- Place the feet between the bottom two layers of the body and use the remaining yarn from the body to sew across the seam, with the feet in between, to close the body and at the same time attach the feet.
- Sew an arm to each side of the body, between Rnd 1 and Rnd 4.
- Sew Rnd 27 of the head to Rnd 1 of the body.

PUG

Puppies love to snuggle in their cozy beds.

DIMENSIONS

12.2 in. (31 cm) long and 6.3 in. (16 cm) wide

MATERIALS

DK #3 lightweight yarn (sample shown in Scheepjes Stone Washed):
- beige (Boulder Opal): 164 yd. (150 m)
- black (Black Onyx): 87.5 yd. (80 m)

Optional: small scrap of red for bow
Crochet hook: US size D-3 (3 mm)
Brown and black safety eyes, 15 mm
Black or brown safety nose, 15 mm wide
Small amount of fiberfill stuffing
Yarn needle and scissors

DIFFICULTY LEVEL

EARS (MAKE 2)

Rnd 1: With black, start with a magic ring, 6sc in the ring. (6)
Rnd 2: Sc1 in each stitch around. (6)
Rnd 3: 2sc in each stitch around. (12)
Rnd 4: *Sc1, 2sc in next*, repeat from * to * around. (18)
Rnd 5: *Sc2, 2sc in next*, repeat from * to * around. (24)
Rnd 6–Rnd 7: Sc1 in each stitch around. (24)
Rnd 8: *Sc2, sc2tog*, repeat from * to * around. (18)
Rnd 9–Rnd 12: Sc1 in each stitch around. (18)
Cut a long tail and don't weave in the ends.

HEAD

Rnd 1: With beige, ch9, take first ear, sc in each of the 18 stitches of first ear, sc in each of the 9 chains you just made, sc in each of the 18 stitches of second ear. (54; this means you'll count first 9 chains, first ear, 9 sc, and second ear)
Note: Keep tails of ears on the outside of the head; you'll use them later.
Rnd 2–Rnd 5: Sc1 in each stitch around. (54)
Rnd 6: Sc10, **with black** sc3, **with beige** sc38, **with black** sc3. (54)
Rnd 7: With beige sc10, **with black** sc4, **with beige** sc37, **with black** sc3. (54)
Rnd 8: With black sc1, **with beige** sc9, **with black** sc5, **with beige** sc36, **with black** sc3. (54)
Rnd 9: With black sc2, **with beige** sc8, **with black** sc9, **with beige** sc29, **with black** sc6. (54)
Rnd 10: With black sc3, **with beige** sc8, **with black** sc9, **with beige** sc28, **with black** sc6. (54)
Rnd 11: With black sc3, **with beige** sc9, **with black** sc8, **with beige** sc29, **with black** sc5. (54)
Rnd 12: With black sc3, **with beige** sc10, **with black** sc7, **with beige** sc30, **with black** sc4. (54)
Rnd 13: With black sc3, **with beige** sc11, **with black** sc6, **with beige** sc31, **with black** sc3. (54)
Rnd 14: With black sc3, **with beige** sc4, sc2tog, *sc7, sc2tog*, repeat from * to * to end. (48)

Cut the black yarn.
Rnd 15: *Sc6, sc2tog*, repeat from * to * around. (42)
Rnd 16: *Sc5, sc2tog*, repeat from * to * around. (36)
On each of the ears you still have a thread hanging; use it to sew through both sides of the ears between Rnd 12 of the ear and Rnd 1 of the head so the ear won't get stuffed. After that, fold the ear like it's folded in the pictures and sew it in place with the remaining yarn, and weave in the remaining ends. Attach safety eyes between Rnd 11 and Rnd 12 of the head.
Rnd 17: *Sc4, sc2tog*, repeat from * to * around. (30)
Rnd 18: *Sc3, sc2tog*, repeat from * to * around. (24)
Rnd 19: *Sc2, sc2tog*, repeat from * to * around. (18)
Stuff the head.
Rnd 20: *Sc1, sc2tog*, repeat from * to * around. (12)
Fold seam flat and sew front and back of the head together; weave in the ends.

NOSE

Rnd 1: With black ch6, sc1 in second ch from hook, sc3, 3sc in last, continue along other side of chains, sc4, 3sc in last. (14)
Rnd 2: *Sc6, 5sc in next*, repeat from * to * around. (22)
Rnd 3: Sc6, 3sc in next, sc8, 3sc in next, sc6. (26)
Rnd 4–Rnd 5: Sc1 in each stitch around. (26)
Cut a long tail, attach safety nose in center of Rnd 3, stuff nose, and sew to head.

BODY

Rnd 1: With beige ch18, 1dc in third ch from hook, dc14, 3dc in last, continue along other side of chains, dc15, 3dc in last, sl st in first dc. (36)
Rnd 2: Ch2 (doesn't count as first stitch for entire pattern), *dc17, 2dc in next*, repeat from * to * one more time, sl st in first dc. (38)
Rnd 3: Ch2, *dc18, 2dc in next*, repeat from * to * one more time, sl st in first dc. (40)
Rnd 4: Ch2, *dc19, 2dc in next*, repeat from * to * one more time, sl st in first dc. (42)
Rnd 5: Ch2, *dc20, 2dc in next*, repeat from * to * one more time, sl st in first dc. (44)
Rnd 6: Ch2, *dc21, 2dc in next*, repeat from * to * one more time, sl st in first dc. (46)
Rnd 7: Ch2, *dc22, 2dc in next*, repeat from * to * one more time, sl st in first dc. (48)
Rnd 8: Ch2, *dc23, 2dc in next*, repeat from * to * one more time, sl st in first dc. (50)
Rnd 9: Ch2, *dc24, 2dc in next*, repeat from * to * one more time, sl st in first dc. (52)
Rnd 10: Ch2, *dc25, 2dc in next*, repeat from * to * one more time, sl st in first dc. (54)
Rnd 11: Ch2, *dc26, 2dc in next*, repeat from * to * one more time, sl st in first dc. (56)
Rnd 12: Ch2, *dc27, 2dc in next*, repeat from * to * one more time, sl st in first dc. (58)
Rnd 13: Ch2, *dc28, 2dc in next*, repeat from * to * one more time, sl st in first dc. (60)
Rnd 14: Ch2, *dc29, 2dc in next*, repeat from * to * one more time, sl st in first dc. (62)
Rnd 15: Ch2, *dc30, 2dc in next*, repeat from * to * one more time, sl st in first dc. (64)
Rnd 16: Ch2, *dc31, 2dc in next*, repeat from * to * one more time, sl st in first dc. (66)
Rnd 17: Ch2, *dc32, 2dc in next*, repeat from * to * one more time, sl st in first dc. (68)
Rnd 18: Ch2, *dc33, 2dc in next*, repeat from * to * one more time, sl st in first dc. (70)
Rnd 19: Ch2, *dc34, 2dc in next*, repeat from * to * one more time, sl st in first dc. (72)
Rnd 20: Ch2, *dc35, 2dc in next*, repeat from * to * one more time, sl st in first dc. (74)
Cut a long tail to close the body in the end.

ARMS (MAKE 2)

Rnd 1: With beige, start with a magic ring, 6sc in the loop. (6)
Rnd 2: 2sc in each stitch around. (12)
Rnd 3: *Sc1, 2sc in next*, repeat from * to * around. (18)
Rnd 4: *Sc2, 2sc in next*, repeat from * to * around. (24)
Rnd 5–Rnd 9: Sc1 in each stitch around. (24)
Rnd 10: *Sc2, sc2tog*, repeat from * to * around. (18)
Rnd 11–Rnd 12: Sc1 in each stitch around. (18)
Rnd 13: Sl st 1, ch2 (doesn't count as first stitch now and throughout), dc1 in each stitch around, sl st in first dc. (18)
Rnd 14: Ch2, dc2tog, dc1 in each stitch around, sl st in first dc. (17)
At this point, stuff the hand (not too much) and use a small piece of yarn to sew across the arm between Rnd 12 and Rnd 13.
Rnd 15: Ch2, dc1 in each stitch around, sl st in first dc. (17)
Rnd 16: Ch2, dc2tog, dc1 in each stitch around, sl st in first dc. (16)
Rnd 17: Ch2, dc1 in each stitch around, sl st in first dc. (16)
Rnd 18: Ch2, dc2tog, dc1 in each stitch around, sl st in first dc. (15)
Rnd 19: Ch2, dc1 in each stitch around, sl st in first dc. (15)
Rnd 20: Ch2, dc2tog, dc1 in each stitch around, sl st in first dc. (14)
Rnd 21: Ch2, dc1 in each stitch around, sl st in first dc. (14)
Rnd 22: Ch2, dc2tog, dc1 in each stitch around, sl st in first dc. (13)
Cut a long tail to attach the arms to the body in the end.

LEGS (MAKE 2)

Rnd 1: With beige, start with a magic ring, ch2, 12dc in the ring, sl st in first dc. (12)
Rnd 2: Ch2, *dc1, 2dc in next*, repeat from * to * around, sl st in first dc. (18)
Rnd 3–Rnd 7: Ch2, dc1 in each stitch around, sl st in first dc. (18)
Cut yarn and weave in the ends.

TAIL

Rnd 1: With beige, start with a magic ring, 6sc in the ring. (6)
Rnd 2: 2sc in each stitch around. (12)
Rnd 3–Rnd 30: Sc1 in each stitch around. (12)
Tie a knot in the tail and weave in the ends.

BOW (OPTIONAL)

With red, start with a magic ring, *ch3, 6tr in the loop, ch3, sl st in ring*, repeat from * to * one more time.
Cut a long tail, wrap it around the center of the bow a few times, and tie a knot on the back of the bow. Leave a tail to attach later.

PUTTING IT ALL TOGETHER

- Place both legs and tail between the bottom two layers of the body. Use the remaining yarn from the body and sew across the seam, with the legs and the tail in between, to close and at the same time attach all parts.
- Sew an arm to each side of the body between Rnd 1 and Rnd 4.
- Sew Rnd 15 of the head (not counting ears) to Rnd 1 of the body.
- Optional: Sew bow to the left ear.

ROBOT

Beep! Beep! Come and see what I can do!

DIMENSIONS

11.8 in. (30 cm) long and 6.3 in. (16 cm) wide

MATERIALS

DK #3 lightweight yarn (sample shown in Scheepjes Stone Washed):
- gray (Smokey Quartz): 164 yd. (150 m)
- black (Black Onyx): 87.5 yd. (80 m)
- blue (Green Agate): 87.5 yd. (80 m)

Crochet hook: US size D-3 (3 mm)
Black and blue safety eyes, 12 mm
Small amount of fiberfill stuffing
Yarn needle and scissors

DIFFICULTY LEVEL

HEAD

Rnd 1: With gray ch21, sc1 in second ch from hook, sc18, 4sc in last, continue along other side of chains, sc18, 4sc in last. (45)

Rnd 2–Rnd 20: Sc1 in each stitch around. (45)

Attach safety eyes between Rnd 12 and Rnd 13 with 9 stitches in between.

Cut a long tail, fold the opening horizontally, and sew the seam half closed. Stuff the head and sew closed to the end.

BODY

Rnd 1: With gray ch18, 1dc in third ch from hook, dc14, 3dc in last, continue along other side of chains, dc15, 3dc in last, sl st in first dc. (36)

Rnd 2: Ch2 (doesn't count as first stitch for entire pattern), *dc17, 2dc in next*, repeat from * to * one more time, sl st in first dc. (38)

Rnd 3: Ch2, *dc18, 2dc in next*, repeat from * to * one more time, sl st in first dc. (40)

Rnd 4: Ch2, *dc19, 2dc in next*, repeat from * to * one more time, sl st in first dc. (42)

Rnd 5: Ch2, dc4, **with blue** dc12, **with gray** dc4, 2dc in next, dc20, 2dc in next, sl st in first dc. (44)

Rnd 6: Ch2, dc4, **with blue** dc13, **with gray** dc4, 2dc in next, dc21, 2dc in next, sl st in first dc. (46)

Rnd 7: Ch2, dc4, **with blue** dc14, **with gray** dc4, 2dc in next, dc22, 2dc in next, sl st in first dc. (48)

Rnd 8: Ch2, dc4, **with blue** dc15, **with gray** dc4, 2dc in next, dc23, 2dc in next, sl st in first dc. (50)

Rnd 9: Ch2, dc4, **with blue** dc16, **with gray** dc4, 2dc in next, dc24, 2dc in next, sl st in first dc. (52)

Rnd 10: Ch2, dc4, **with blue** dc17, **with gray** dc4, 2dc in next, dc25, 2dc in next, sl st in first dc. (54)

Rnd 11: Ch2, dc4, **with blue** dc3, **with gray** dc12, **with blue** dc3, **with gray** dc4, 2dc in next, dc26, 2dc in next, sl st in first dc. (56)

Rnd 12: Ch2, dc4, **with blue** dc2, **with gray** dc2, **with blue** dc11, **with gray** dc2, **with blue** dc2, **with gray** dc4, 2dc in next, dc27, 2dc in next, sl st in first dc. (58)
Rnd 13: Ch2, dc4, **with blue** dc2, **with gray** dc2, **with blue** dc12, **with gray** dc2, **with blue** dc2, **with gray** dc4, 2dc in next, dc28, 2dc in next, sl st in first dc. (60)
Rnd 14: Ch2, dc4, **with blue** dc2, **with gray** dc2, **with blue** dc13, **with gray** dc2, **with blue** dc2, **with gray** dc4, 2dc in next, dc29, 2dc in next, sl st in first dc. (62)
Rnd 15: Ch2, dc4, **with blue** dc2, **with gray** dc2, **with blue** dc14, **with gray** dc2, **with blue** dc2, **with gray** dc4, 2dc in next, dc30, 2dc in next, sl st in first dc. (64)
Cut the blue yarn.
Rnd 16: Ch2, *dc31, 2dc in next*, repeat from * to * one more time, sl st in first dc. (66)
Rnd 17: Ch2, *dc32, 2dc in next*, repeat from * to * one more time, sl st in first dc. (68)
Rnd 18: Ch2, *dc33, 2dc in next*, repeat from * to * one more time, sl st in first dc. (70)

Rnd 19: Ch2, *dc34, 2dc in next*, repeat from * to * one more time, sl st in first dc. (72)
Rnd 20: Ch2, *dc35, 2dc in next*, repeat from * to * one more time, sl st in first dc. (72)
Cut a long tail to close the body in the end.

ARMS (MAKE 2)

Rnd 1: With gray, start with a magic ring, 6sc in the ring. (6)
Rnd 2: 2sc in each stitch around. (12)
Rnd 3: *Sc1, 2sc in next*, repeat from * to * around. (18)
Rnd 4–Rnd 9: Sc1 in each stitch around. (18)
Rnd 10: With black sl st 1, ch1 (doesn't count as first stitch, now and throughout), sc1 in each stitch around, sl st in first sc. (18)
Rnd 11: With gray ch2, dc2tog, dc1 in each stitch around, sl st in first dc. (17)
Stuff the hand and sew across the arm between Rnd 9 and Rnd 10.
Rnd 12: Ch2, dc1 in each stitch around, sl st in first dc. (17)
Rnd 13: Ch2, dc2tog, dc1 in each stitch around, sl st in first dc. (16)
Rnd 14: With black ch1, sc1 in each stitch around, sl st in first sc. (16)
Rnd 15: With gray ch2, dc2tog, dc1 in each stitch around, sl st in first dc. (15)
Rnd 16: Ch2, dc1 in each stitch around, sl st in first dc. (15)
Rnd 17: Ch2, dc2tog, dc1 in each stitch around, sl st in first dc. (14)
Rnd 18: With black ch1, sc1 in each stitch around, sl st in first sc. (14)
Rnd 19: With gray ch2, dc2tog, dc1 in each stitch around, sl st in first dc. (13)
Rnd 20: Ch2, dc1 in each stitch around, sl st in first dc. (13)
Cut a long tail to attach the arms to the body in the end.

FEET (MAKE 2)

Rnd 1: With black, start with a magic ring, 6sc in the ring. (6)
Rnd 2: 2sc in each stitch around. (12)
Rnd 3: *Sc1, 2sc in next*, repeat from * to * around. (18)
Rnd 4–Rnd 9: Sc1 in each stitch around. (18)
Cut tail, weave in ends, and stuff feet lightly.

EARS (MAKE 2)

Rnd 1: With black, start with a magic ring, 6sc in the ring. (6)
Rnd 2: 2sc in each stitch around. (12)
Rnd 3: *Sc1, 2sc in next*, repeat from * to * around. (18)
Rnd 4–Rnd 5: Sc1 in each stitch around. (18)
Cut a long tail to attach the ears to the head later; stuff lightly.

ANTENNA

Rnd 1: With blue, start with a magic ring, 6sc in the ring. (6)
Rnd 2: 2sc in each stitch around. (12)
Rnd 3: Sc1 in each stitch around. (12)
Cut tail and stuff the top.
Rnd 4: With black sc2tog 6 times. (6)
Rnd 5–Rnd 8: Sc1 in each stitch around. (6)
Cut a long tail to attach to the head in the end.

PUTTING IT ALL TOGETHER

- Start by putting together the head: Sew an ear to each side of the head between Rnd 6 and Rnd 15. Sew the antenna to the top of the head.
- With black yarn, embroider a graph on the top screen of the robot and an indicator on the bottom screen. I like to embroider by first making the entire line and then going backward through the line as shown in the picture.
- Place the feet between the bottom two layers of the body and use the remaining yarn from the body to sew across the seam, with the feet in between, to close the body and at the same time attach the feet.
- Sew an arm to each side of the body, between Rnd 1 and Rnd 4.
- Sew Rnd 17 of the head to Rnd 1 of the body.

UNICORN

Join me in the land where dreams come true!

DIMENSIONS

14.6 in. (37 cm) long and 6.7 in. (17 cm) wide

MATERIALS

DK #3 lightweight yarn (sample shown in Scheepjes Stone Washed):
- pink (Corondum Ruby): 164 in. (150 m)
- white (Moon Stone): 109.4 in. (100 m)
- black (Black Onyx): 54.7 in. (50 m)
- yellow (Yellow Jasper): 32.8 in. (30 m)
- various colors for the mane

Crochet hook: US size D-3 (3 mm)
Brown and black safety eyes, 15 mm
Black safety eyes, 10 mm (for nostrils)
Small amount of fiberfill stuffing
Yarn needle and scissors

DIFFICULTY LEVEL

INSTRUCTIONS

To make the unicorn, follow the instructions for the horse on pages 107–9, but replace beige with pink yarn and add a few strands of different colors into the mane. Finally, hook the horn as follows to complete the unicorn.

HORN

Rnd 1: With yellow, start with a magic ring, 6sc in the ring. (6)
Rnd 2: Sc1 in each stitch around. (6)
Rnd 3: 2sc in each stitch around. (12)
Rnd 4–Rnd 5: Sc1 in each stitch around. (12)
Rnd 6: *Sc1, 2sc in next*, repeat from * to * around. (18)
Rnd 7–Rnd 11: Sc1 in each stitch around. (18)
Cut a long tail, stuff the horn, and sew the horn to the forehead from Rnd 3 to Rnd 8.

CLOTHES FOR YOUR DOLLS

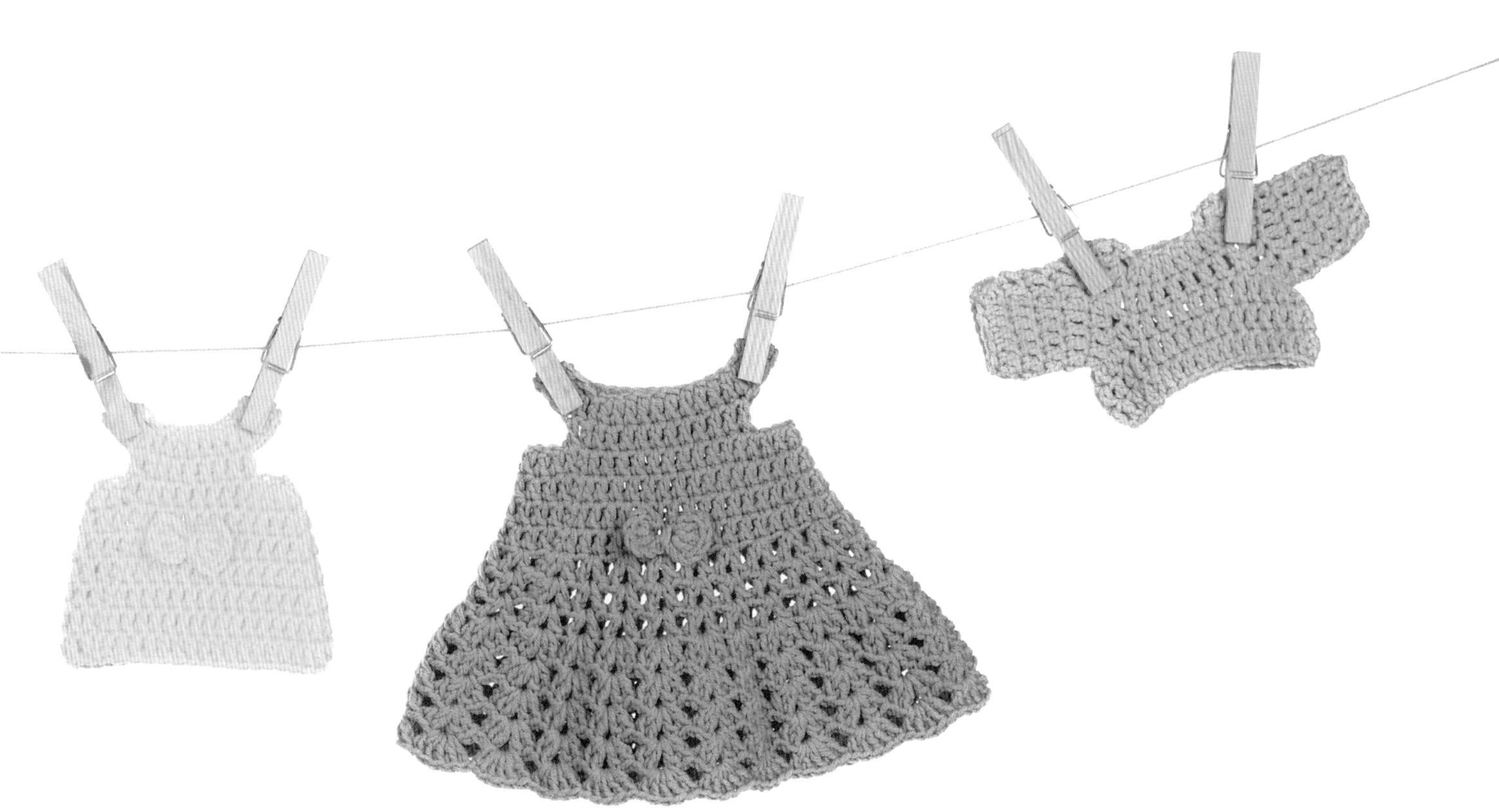

CLOTHES FOR THE RAGDOLLS

These ragdolls also want to look extra cute occasionally, so crochet them a few special pieces to wear!

MATERIALS

- DK weight yarn. I used Scheepjes Soft Fun (different colors); each item of clothing can be hooked with 1 ball (140 m)
- Crochet hook: US size G-6 (4 mm)
- Yarn needle and scissors

SPECIAL STITCHES

- V-stitch (v-st) = dc, ch1, dc in same stitch
- Double v-stitch = 2dc, ch1, 2dc in same stitch

DIFFICULTY LEVEL

PINK DRESS

(FITS STANDARD-SIZE DOLL)

Rnd 1: Ch30, sl st in the first ch to form a ring. Ch2 (does not count as the first stitch here and throughout), *dc10, 3dc in the next stitch, dc3, 3dc in the next stitch*, repeat from * to * once more, sl st in the first dc. (38)
Rnd 2: Ch2, dc11, ch8, skip 7 dc, dc12, ch8, skip 7 dc, dc1, sl st in first dc. (40)
Rnd 3: Ch2, dc1 in each stitch around, sl st in first dc. (40)
Rnd 4: Ch2, dc15, 2dc in next stitch, dc19, 2dc in next stitch, dc4, sl st in first dc. (42)
Rnd 5: Ch2, dc16, 2dc in next stitch, dc10, [Bow: ch4, 3dc in first of ch4, ch3, sl st in same as 3dc, ch3, 3dc in same as 3dc, ch3, sl st in same as 3dc], 10dc, 2dc in next stitch, dc4, sl st in first dc. (44)
Rnd 6: Ch2, dc17, 2dc in next stitch, dc10, dc1 around the center of the bow in the stitch below, dc10, 2dc in next stitch, dc4, sl st in first dc. (46)
Rnd 7: Ch2, 1 v-st in same as ch2, skip 1 dc, *1 v-st in next dc, skip 1 dc*, repeat from * to * around, sl st in first dc of first v-st. (23 v-st)
Rnd 8–Rnd 9: Sl st in the ch-1 space of the first v-st, ch2, 1 v-st in same as ch2, 1 v-st in ch-1 space of each v-st around, sl st in first dc of first v-st. (23 v-st)
Rnd 10: Sl st in ch-1 space of the first v-st, ch2, 1 double v-st in same as ch2, 1 double v-st in ch-1 space of each v-st around, sl st in first dc of first double v-st. (23 double v-st)
Rnd 11–Rnd 13: Sl st in ch-1 space of the first double v-st, ch2, 1 double v-st in same as ch2, 1 double v-st in ch-1 space of every double v-st around, sl st in first dc of first double v-st. (23 double v-st)
Rnd 14: Sl st in ch-1 space of the first double v-st, ch2, 5dc in same as ch2, 5dc in ch-1 space of each double v-st around, sl st in first dc. (23 groups of 5dc)
Cut the yarn and weave in the ends.

RED DRESS

(FITS STANDARD-SIZE DOLL)

Rnd 1: Ch30, sl st in first ch to make a ring. Ch2 (doesn't count as first stitch now and throughout), *dc10, 3dc in next stitch, dc3, 3dc in next stitch*, repeat from * to * once more, sl st in first dc. (38)

Rnd 2: Ch2, dc11, ch8, skip 7 dc, dc12, ch8, skip 7 dc, dc1, sl st in first dc. (40)

Rnd 3: Ch2, dc1 in each stitch around, sl st in first dc. (40)

Rnd 4: Ch2, dc15, 2dc in next stitch, dc19, 2dc in next stitch, dc4, sl st in first dc. (42)

Rnd 5: Ch2, dc16, 2dc in next stitch, dc10, [Bow: ch4, 3dc in first of ch4, ch3, sl st in same as 3dc, ch3, 3dc in same as 3dc, ch3, sl st in same as 3dc], dc10, 2dc in next stitch, dc4, sl st in first dc. (44)

Rnd 6: Ch2, dc17, 2dc in next stitch, dc10, dc1 around the center of the bow in the stitch below, dc10, 2dc in next stitch, dc4, sl st in first dc. (46)

Rnd 7: Ch2, dc18, 2dc in next stitch, dc22, 2dc in next stitch, dc4, sl st in first dc. (48)

Rnd 8: Ch2, dc19, 2dc in next stitch, dc23, 2dc in next stitch, dc4, sl st in first dc. (50)

Rnd 9: Ch2, dc20, 2dc in next stitch, dc24, 2dc in next stitch, dc4, sl st in first dc. (52)

Rnd 10: Ch2, dc21, 2dc in next stitch, dc25, 2dc in next stitch, dc4, sl st in first dc. (54)

Rnd 11: Ch2, dc22, 2dc in next stitch, dc26, 2dc in next stitch, dc4, sl st in first dc. (56)

Rnd 12: Ch2, dc23, 2dc in next stitch, dc27, 2dc in next stitch, dc4, sl st in first dc. (58)

Rnd 13: Ch2, dc24, 2dc in next stitch, dc28, 2dc in next stitch, dc4, sl st in first dc. (60)

Rnd 14: Ch2, dc25, 2dc in next stitch, dc29, 2dc in next stitch, dc4, sl st in first dc. (62)

Rnd 15: Ch2, dc26, 2dc in next stitch, dc30, 2dc in next stitch, dc4, sl st in first dc. (64)

Rnd 16: Ch2, dc27, 2dc in next stitch, dc31, 2dc in next stitch, dc4, sl st in first dc. (66)

Cut yarn and weave in ends.

PEACH DRESS

(FITS MINI DOLL)

Rnd 1: Ch20, sl st in first ch to make a ring. Ch2 (doesn't count as first stitch now and throughout), *dc6, 3dc in next stitch, dc2, 3dc in next stitch*, repeat from * to * once more, sl st in first dc. (28)

Rnd 2: Ch2, dc7, ch7, skip 6 dc, dc8, ch7, skip 6 dc, dc1, sl st in first dc. (30)

Rnd 3: Ch2, dc1 in each stitch around, sl st in first dc. (30)

Rnd 4: Ch2, dc10, 2dc in next stitch, dc7, [Bow: ch4, 3dc in first of ch4, ch3, sl st in same as 3dc, ch3, 3dc in same as 3dc, ch3, sl st in same as 3dc], dc7, 2dc in next stitch, dc4, sl st in first dc. (32)

Rnd 5: Ch2, dc11, 2dc in next stitch, dc7, dc1 around the center of the bow in the stitch below, dc7, 2dc in next stitch, dc4, sl st in first dc. (34)

Rnd 6: Ch2, 1 v-st in same as ch2, skip 1 dc, *1 v-st in next dc, skip 1 dc*, repeat from * to * around, sl st in first dc of first v-st. (17 v-st)

Rnd 7: Sl st in the ch1-space of the first v-st, ch2, 1 v-st in same as ch2, 1 v-st in the ch1-space of each v-st around, sl st in first dc of first v-st. (17 v-st)

Rnd 8: Sl st in the ch1-space of the first v-st, ch2, 1 double v-st in same as ch2, 1 double v-st in the ch1-space of each v-st around, sl st in first dc of first double v-st. (17 double v-st)

Rnd 9: Sl st in the ch1-space of the first double v-st, ch2, 5dc in same as ch2, 5dc in the ch1-space of each double v-st around, sl st in first dc. (17 groups of 5dc)

Cut yarn and weave in ends.

YELLOW DRESS

(FITS MINI DOLL)

Rnd 1: Ch20, sl st in first ch to make a ring. Ch2 (doesn't count as first stitch now and throughout), *dc6, 3dc in next stitch, dc2, 3dc in next stitch*, repeat from * to * once more, sl st in first dc. (28)
Rnd 2: Ch2, dc7, ch7, skip 6 dc, dc8, ch7, skip 6 dc, dc1, sl st in first dc. (30)
Rnd 3: Ch2, dc1 in each stitch around, sl st in first dc. (30)
Rnd 4: Ch2, dc10, 2dc in next stitch, dc7, [Bow: ch4, 3dc in first of ch4, ch3, sl st in same as 3dc, ch3, 3dc in same as 3dc, ch3, sl st in same as 3dc], dc7, 2dc in next stitch, dc4, sl st in first dc. (32)
Rnd 5: Ch2, dc11, 2dc in next stitch, dc7, dc1 around the center of the bow in the stitch below, dc7, 2dc in next stitch, dc4, sl st in first dc. (34)
Rnd 6: Ch2, dc12, 2dc in next stitch, dc16, 2dc in next stitch, dc4, sl st in first dc. (36)
Rnd 7: Ch2, dc13, 2dc in next stitch, dc17, 2dc in next stitch, dc4, sl st in first dc. (38)
Rnd 8: Ch2, dc14, 2dc in next stitch, dc18, 2dc in next stitch, dc4, sl st in first dc. (40)
Rnd 9: Ch2, dc15, 2dc in next stitch, dc19, 2dc in next stitch, dc4, sl st in first dc. (42)
Cut yarn and weave in ends.

DARK BLUE SWEATER

(FITS STANDARD-SIZE DOLL)
Rnd 1: Ch30, sl st in first ch to make a ring. Ch2 (doesn't count as first stitch now and throughout), *dc10, 3dc in nextstitch, dc3, 3dc in next stitch*, repeat from * to * once more, sl st in first dc. (38)
Rnd 2: Ch2, dc11, ch8, skip 7 dc, dc12, ch8, skip 7 dc, dc1, sl st in first dc. (40)
Rnd 3: Ch2, dc14, 2dc in next stitch, dc19, 2dc in next stitch, dc5, sl st in first dc. (42)
Rnd 4: Ch2, dc15, 2dc in next stitch, dc20, 2dc in next stitch, dc5, sl st in first dc. (44)
Rnd 5: Ch2, dc16, 2dc in next stitch, dc21, 2dc in next stitch, dc5, sl st in first dc. (46)
Rnd 6: Ch2, dc17, 2dc in next stitch, dc22, 2dc in next stitch, dc5, sl st in first dc. (48)
Rnd 7: Ch2, dc18, 2dc in next stitch, dc23, 2dc in next stitch, dc5, sl st in first dc. (50)
Rnd 8: Ch2, dc19, 2dc in next stitch, dc24, 2dc in next stitch, dc5, sl st in first dc. (52)
Cut yarn and weave in ends.

SLEEVES (MAKE 2)
Rnd 1: Attach yarn in the first ch of Rnd 2. Ch2 (doesn't count as first stitch now and throughout), dc8, dc1 in the side of the next dc of Rnd 2, continue in the skipped stitch of Rnd 1: dc7, dc1 in the side of the next dc of Rnd 2, sl st in first dc. (17)
Rnd 2–Rnd 7: Ch2, dc1 in each stitch around, sl st in first dc. (17)
Cut yarn and weave in ends. Repeat for second sleeve.

LIGHT BLUE SWEATER

(FITS MINI DOLL)

Rnd 1: Ch20, sl st in first ch to make a ring. Ch2 (doesn't count as first stitch now and throughout), *dc6, 3dc in next stitch, dc2, 3dc in next stitch*, repeat from * to * once more, sl st in first dc. (28)

Rnd 2: Ch2, dc7, ch7, skip 6 dc, dc8, ch7, skip 6 dc, dc1, sl st in first dc. (30)

Rnd 3: Ch2, dc10, 2dc in next stitch, dc14, 2dc in next stitch, dc4, sl st in first dc. (32)

Rnd 4: Ch2, dc11, 2dc in next stitch, dc15, 2dc in next stitch, dc4, sl st in first dc. (34)

Rnd 5: Ch2, dc12, 2dc in next stitch, dc16, 2dc in next stitch, dc4, sl st in first dc. (36)

Cut yarn and weave in ends.

SLEEVES (MAKE 2)

Rnd 1: Attach yarn in the first ch of Rnd 2, ch2 (doesn't count as first stitch now and throughout), dc7, dc1 in the side of the next dc of Rnd 2, continue in the skipped stitch of Rnd 1: dc6, dc1 in the side of the next dc of Rnd 2, sl st in first dc. (15)

Rnd 2–Rnd 5: Ch2, dc1 in each stitch around, sl st in first dc. (15)

Cut yarn and weave in ends. Repeat for second sleeve.

ACKNOWLEDGMENTS

Wow, my third book has already been delivered, made possible of course by a lot of lovely people whom I would like to thank! First of all, my wonderful family: Josse, you always provide inspiration and a smile in moments of lack thereof. Dear Mijntje and Julia, you are beautifully photographed again. I am very proud of you!

Ans Baart has not only tested the patterns and checked for errors but also crocheted the fantastic frog variations when I was unable to do that myself. Thank you for always being there for me, and more than that! My dear parents, parents-in-law, brothers, sisters-in-law, family, friends, and colleagues who still have no idea what it is all about, but who are always interested in listening to my adventures in the handicraft world.

The fantastic ladies who tested the patterns: Colette Hendriks, Bianca van den Maarel, Ester Zweers, Karin Frenzen, Eveline Hartog, Monique Schut, Diane van Lier-Noordenbos, Corina van Krieken, Eveline Koeleman, Esther Emaar, Tine Oetzman, Joke Mate, Dennis de Gussem, and Arianne Schenkelaars-Verberne. And my English version pattern testers: Emily Truman, Lindsey Mae Strippelhoff, Sandy Yurkins Powers, Susan Higbe, Annie Shelton, Leslie Mansfield, Erin Medley, Lanie Brown, Heather Hoffman, Melanie Joy Pizzini, Malonie Ellingson, Brittney Ragon, Lindsey Lively, Mandy Jo, Kimberly Rose, Debbie Allen Richardson, Yee Wong, and Morea Peterson.

Thank you, Debby Bergmeester, for setting up the ragdoll group and your enthusiasm! Peggy Jansen-Peters, also thanks for your support and contribution!

Thank you, G. Brouwer & Zn Fournituren Groothandel, de Bondt BV, and Jeanet Jaffari-Schroevers from Atelier Jaffari. And finally, the wonderful employees of Kosmos.

Thank you very much for your support and trust!

VISUAL INDEX

ANIMAL FAMILIES

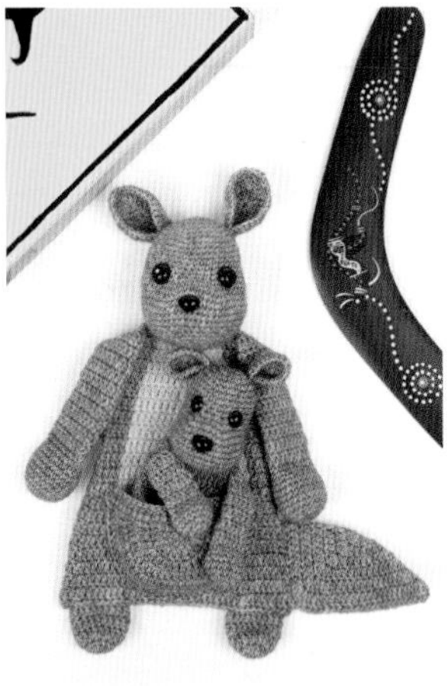

Kangaroo 55

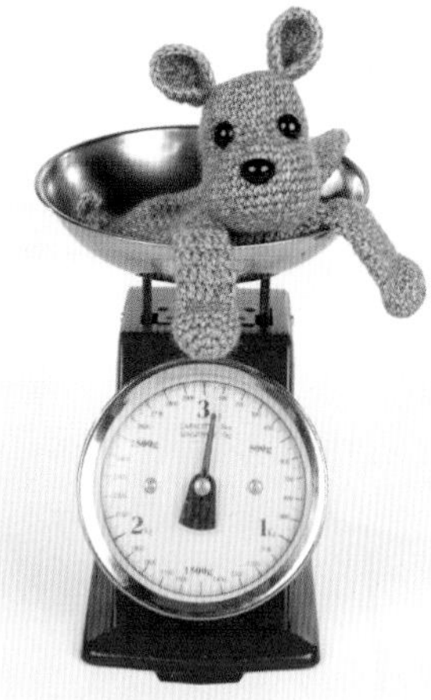

Joey 61

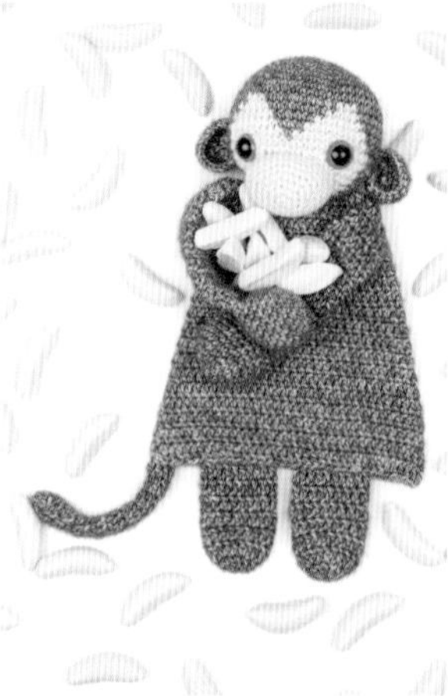

Monkey 65

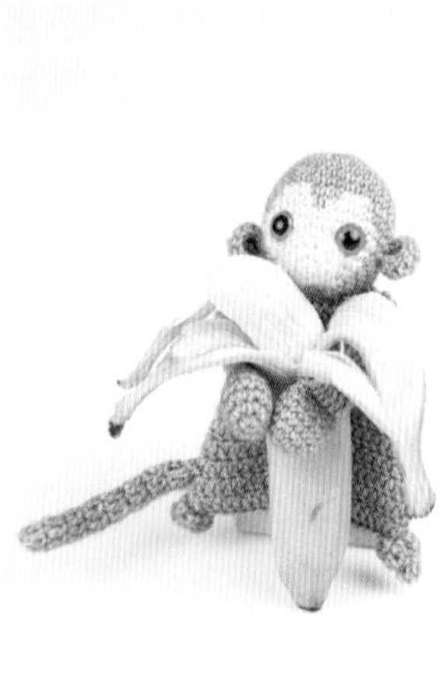

Baby Monkey 68

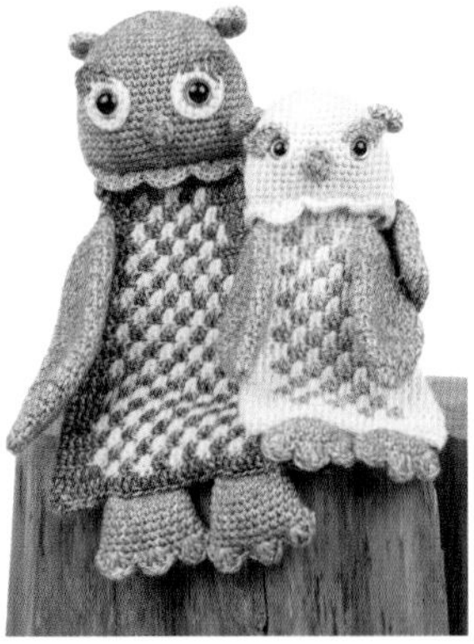

Owl 73

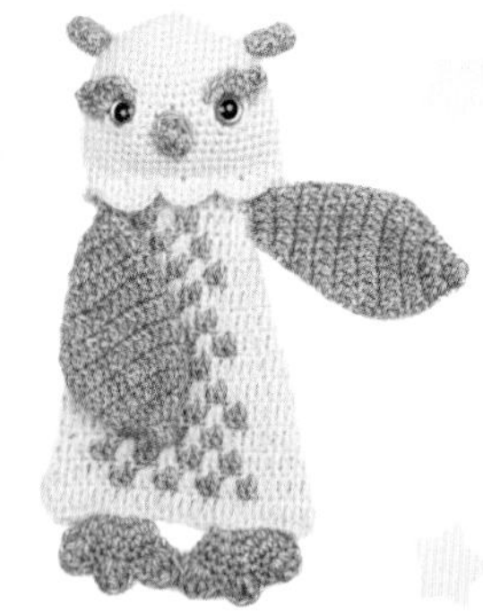

Owlet 77

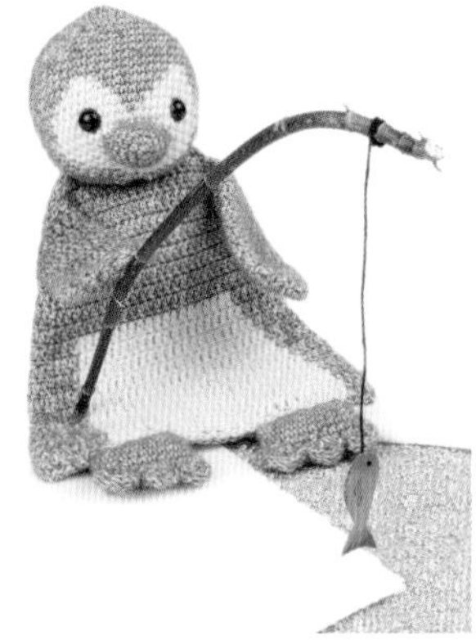

Penguin 81

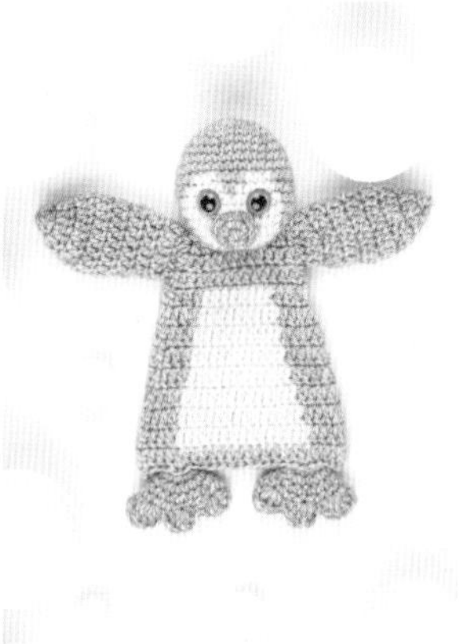

Baby Penguin 85

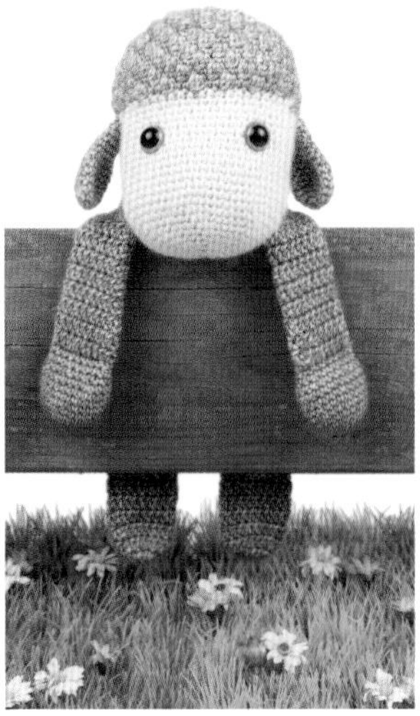

Sheep 89

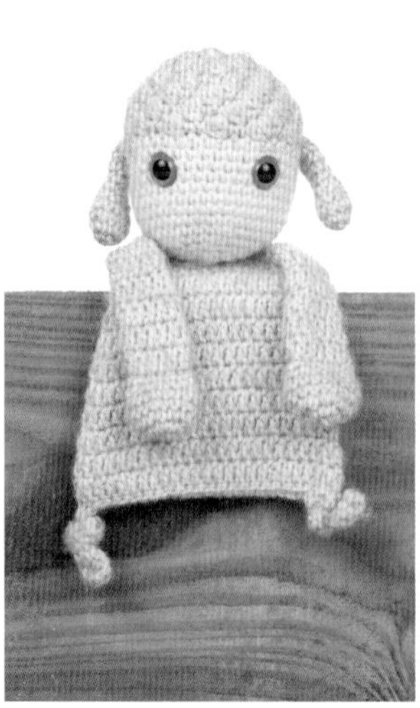

Lamb 93

OTHER ANIMALS AND FRIENDS

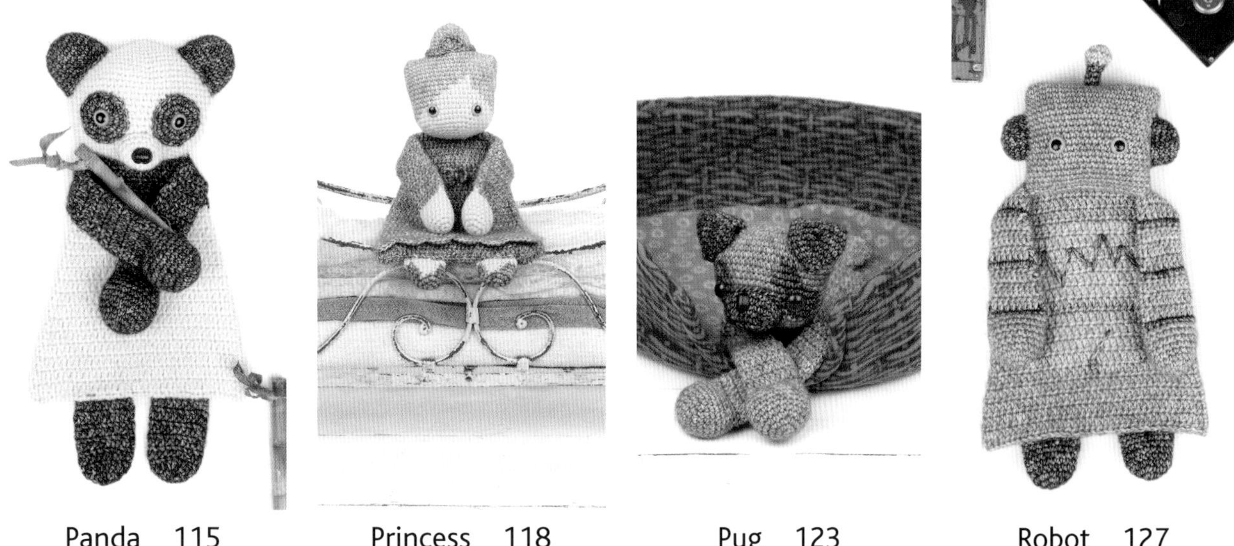

CLOTHES FOR YOUR DOLLS